The Pearl of Great Price

Also by Martin Israel and published by SPCK:
Living Alone (1982)
The Discipline of Love (1985)

The Pearl
of Great Price

A Journey to the Kingdom

Martin Israel

First published in Great Britain 1988
SPCK
Holy Trinity Church
Marylebone Road
London NW1 4DU

British Library Cataloguing in Publication Data

Israel, Martin
    The pearl of great price: a journey to the Kingdom
    1. Christian Life
    I. Title
    248.4   BV4501.2

    ISBN 0-281-04331-0

Phototypesetting by Hart-Talbot Printers Ltd, Saffron Walden
Printed in Great Britain

Dedicated to the memory of
Geoffrey Curtis CR

I have seen the sun break through
to illuminate a small field
for a while, and gone my way
and forgotten it. But that was the pearl
of great price, the one field that had
the treasure in it. I realise now
that I must give all that I have
to possess it. Life is not hurrying

on to a receding future, nor hankering after
an imagined past. It is the turning
aside like Moses to the miracle
of the lit bush, to a brightness
that seemed as transitory as your youth
once, but is the eternity that awaits you.

The Bright Field *by R S Thomas*

This Pearl of Eternity is, First, the Light and Spirit
of God within Thee.
Secondly, This Pearl of Eternity is the Wisdom and
Love of God within Thee.
Thirdly, This Pearl of Eternity is the Church, or
Temple of God within Thee.
Fourthly, and Lastly, This Pearl of Eternity is the
Peace and Joy of God within Thee.

from The Spirit of Prayer *by William Law*

Contents

Acknowledgements

Thanks are due to the following for permission to reproduce copyright material:

Faber and Faber Ltd and Harcourt Brace Jovanovich Inc., for the extracts from 'The Hollow Men' and 'East Coker', from *Collected Poems 1909-1962* by T. S. Eliot. Macmillan Ltd, for the extract from 'The Bright Field', from *Laboratories of the Spirit* by R. S. Thomas.

Prologue

The kingdom of heaven is like treasure buried in a field. The man who found it, buried it again; and for sheer joy went and sold everything he had, and bought that field.
Here is another picture of the kingdom of heaven. A merchant looking out for fine pearls found one of special value, so he went and sold everything he had and bought it (Matthew 13.44-6).

The feature that these two Parables of the Kingdom share is the personal renunciation needed to acquire the precious article; it cannot simply be seized, but has to be left alone until the time when the purchaser is ready to use it properly. If it were acquired without a sacrifice its value would be lowered in the eyes of the seeker and soon it would be defiled. It is a rule that, for most of us, the price adds to the value of an article; only an aware person can fully appreciate a gift. Our health is taken for granted until we have survived a serious illness, just as a true friend may be discovered only when someone, whom we had barely noticed, comes to our aid quite spontaneously in a time of trouble, while those on whom we had relied reveal their ineffectiveness. In the search for the precious pearl the seeker is led into strange adventures, in the course of which he must be ready to yield everything on which his life had previously depended: material security, emotional relationships, religious conviction that is usually identified with faith, reputation, and finally his life itself.

It follows that this awe-inspiring theme tends inexorably to chart the course of the seeker from the first glimpse to the threshold of the great prize. It is a spiritual journey that is being recorded and the theme cannot but assume something of a practical account of spiritual direction as the aspirant is guided day by day. The great saints are the beacons on the path, but we must beware of the temptation of trimming our own particular personality to theirs even to the extent of belittling or disparaging our own special gifts. As we progress on the path, so the precious pearl changes its situation: we see it in a progressively more personal light. Our quest changes us so that we become more precious in our own integrity, and the pearl assumes the nature of an inner light as well as a distant destination.

When we are healed of inner disorder, we ourselves can provide the chalice into which the wine of God may be poured. The wine itself is changed into the person of Christ, whose sacred heart is the pearl. To its precincts we proceed with awe and quiet joy. In the end we find the pearl in our own hearts as we give of ourselves in love to serve the world around us.

1 Intimations

The struggling human form painfully ascends the hill of mortal aspiration, surrounded by multitudes of his own kind. He grasps for the substance of life in a dark, enclosed space. He, like the others, is impelled onward by a deep yearning for life, yet the existence he knows is more akin to a steady, monotonous stamping than to purposeful progress. Within him lies the means of survival and procreation, but he often pursues the unceasingly onward course more out of blind habit than a positive appreciation of the world around him. Yet, in the dark obscurity of life's pageant, a pageant that has its time of exultation and happiness but which proceeds inexorably towards the valley of extinction, he exercises his gift of thought. As Pascal remarked, 'Man is only a reed, the weakest thing in nature, but he is a thinking reed'. Indeed, his contemporary, Descartes, found the proof of a specifically human existence in man's ability to think. He reflects on the past and plans the future in the present moment, but all too often that present moment passes him by unnoticed and unattended to.

Thought diverts him from the present, but no matter how stimulating it may be, thinking soon reaches its own end, its tragic limitation in a world of decay and death; and so the struggling human form learns to divert his thoughts to his immediate tangible environment, to his desires, expectations, emotional needs and fantasies. But all the while this edifice of comforting reflection is being undermined by a subterranean inflow of subversive dread that chills the heart as it casts its shadow on the prospect ahead. It reminds him of his guilt, his fear of exposure and retribution, of the underlying transience of all material achievement, swallowed up, as it must be, by the relentless inroads of ageing and death. Thus the obsessive tendency to superficial thinking finds its own check as a world of darkness limits all expansive plans for the future. The writer of the Book of Ecclesiastes saw starkly the vanity and the essential emptiness that lay at the foundation of all human

1

achievement, and that loomed large as the destiny of all created things. When one looks down on an army of ants moving from one corner of a room to the other, one can see in advance the wall that is to check their journey. But the human is so often oblivious of the wall of mortality that is destined to end his own exertions, despite the power that distinguishes his witness and at first promises so much satisfaction. The end is disillusion and bitter disappointment. If the person had been more aware, he would have seen the 'writing on the wall' and made an alternative plan of direction and development in a murky, unsatisfactory life. Yet all the schemes of the distraught human mind founder on the rocks of the sea of illusion, and man returns to his place of origin, defeated and humiliated.

A world without over-all purpose is dark and menacing. The bent, humourless humans hurry onwards to a place that is both nowhere and everywhere at the same time. The more change engendered on a human level, the less advancement is registered spiritually.

> The sun rises and the sun goes down; back it returns to its place and rises there again. The wind blows south, the wind blows north, round and round it goes and returns full circle. All streams run into the sea, yet the sea never overflows; back to the place from which the streams run they return to run again (Ecclesiastes 1.5-7).

Then from the very heart of the darkness, the very centre of the vanity of existence, a ray of light shines forth. It strikes the heart of the dismal plodder, making him wake up to the reality of the present moment, seeing it as a thing in its own right. At once hope breaks into a closed consciousness, and the blind man is suddenly endowed with the priceless gift of sight. This is the essential human condition: the feet on the solid earth of dreary subsistence with the head in a fog that is shot through with the fire of meaning coming to the mind as isolated sparks that can be allowed either to peter out or else ignite a fire within that transforms the person. 'The light shines on in the dark, and the darkness has never mastered it' (John 1.5), for the ultimate being is light, and in him there is no darkness at all (1 John 1.5).

The Parable of the Sower and the Seed (Matthew 13.4-8) is especially relevant in this context. The seed, the ray of light, falls on the soil of the inner man, the true self, or soul, that is the arbiter of moral values, and there it makes its impression. But in some the light is quickly extinguished by the indifferent spiritual milieu of the surrounding world. In others it bursts into an immediate flame, only to flicker to extinction under the stress and disillusion of everyday life. In yet others its frail ray is continuously outshone by the meretricious glow of earthly diversions, so that it gradually fades from view as the false light, which is in essence the glitter of the forces of darkness, occupies the whole scene. But in a few the spark ignites a delicate flame that persists in the power of its own light, despite all temptations to yield to the seductive blandishments of the world. As a consequence the flame expands slowly into a glowing fire that both consumes the errors of the past and shows the way towards a new realm of values whose peak is the vision of God. The man painfully ascending the mountain of existence, when he sees the light and acknowledges its authenticity, has now to make his decision. Is he to turn his back on it and return to the heedless, purposeless way of the past? Or is he to set his face in the shaft of that light and move away from the glitter of worldly values to attain a vision of God? This is a vision momentarily outlined in the flicker of the illumination, but to be known and treasured by a new life, whose end is the raising of the whole creation to an encounter with God's transfiguring love.

But how is this ray of divine light recognized? It comes suddenly, like a thief in the night, lighting up the flagging consciousness of the person, so that a warmth ignites his heart while a cool breeze caresses his head. 'The people who dwell in darkness have seen a great light: light has dawned upon them, dwellers in a land as dark as death' (Isaiah 9.2). In this beautiful passage Isaiah continues that God has increased his people's joy and given them great gladness, so that they rejoice at harvest. In the light of God, the man toiling at his work, climbing laboriously the upward path of trial and uncertainty, suddenly feels the burden of life, including the draining emotional emanations of those around him, lift from his shoulders, so that for the first time in his experience he knows freedom. This is the freedom to be himself, an individual apart from the mass of humanity, while remaining an essential part of it. It is a spiritual truth that we attain a knowledge of our own unique identity most radiantly when we work with self-transcending devotion in the greater world around us. 'Come to me, all whose work is hard, whose load is heavy, and I will give you relief' (Matthew 11.28). In fact, he comes to us, and when we receive him, he lifts our burden from us by sharing it with us, so that the strength afforded us can in the future be used with an awareness that shows itself in dedicated responsibility.

But the ray of divine illumination is not merely a sensation of inner warmth, a feeling of living presence. It is also coolly directive. In a brief encounter it gives a preview of what one may become, something of a full person created afresh in the image of God, something of Christ himself, but now incarnated in one's own particular name. The divine essence works through disarmingly ordinary people. By contrast, an intellectual or esoteric élite who appear to know much on a theoretical level often fail to register its presence in their lives. The objective proof of a meeting with the divine is an outpouring of love that is the source of all healing. It may start its work among individuals but soon becomes communal in range.

'It is a terrible thing to fall into the hands of the living God' (Hebrews 10.31), for then a higher demand is made on one, a demand that cannot be ignored or evaded. The inescapable call to action follows the vision: there must be growth into integrity and a capacity for serving the world. This is the intimation of the pearl of great price deeply set, and as yet inaccessible, in the mist of eternity. There is no escape from responsive action towards the holy life, for the inner eye has sensed something far more potent than even human grandeur at its most august. This is the glory of a human being, to be able to respond to the divine initiative and traverse the uphill path of integration whose end is sanctification. It is the power of the divine that makes us truly human: the glory of God is a living man as St Irenaeus puts it. The ultimate proof of God is a personal one: the experience of the divine fire that will not let one alone until one has actualized one's full potential. At first that potential may be seen, indeed experienced, in material terms of worldly success, eminence and riches, but as the divine intimation fires the aspiration of the soul, so will no destination other than the vision of God suffice.

When the light is seen and acknowledged, when its authority is accepted, nothing will satisfy, except the possession of that light. This is in its own way a variation on the theme of human love; the lover possesses the beloved and he is filled with joy. But possession, like possessions themselves, has a sadly transient glow. What starts its life as heaven soon attains an infernal power if it cannot be left alone, indeed finally relinquished. This is because it, in a subtle way, separates the lover from the greater experience of humanity by concentrating his rapt attention on one object to the virtual exclusion of all else. Jesus goes so far as to tell his would-be disciples that they have first to hate their most intimate family, even their own lives, before they can truly follow him (Luke 14.26). Admittedly the language of hyperbole modifies the 'hatred' demanded against parents, husbands, wives and children, and brothers and sisters, but the underlying truth is clear enough: the great quest demands total renunciation, at least as an act of faith, in somewhat the same way as Abraham was prepared to sacrifice his beloved son Isaac as a proof of his primary obedience to God, the ultimate Father. All this is hard, virtually impossible, to the man of flesh, but he is being drawn into the path of self-transcendence as he yields his own desires to something too immense to conceive with the naked intellect.

The frail light is the very presence of God, like the 'still, small voice' (or the sound of a gentle breeze), that informed Elijah of what was destined to be (1 Kings 19.13). It is gentle and courteous in its address, but its import is terrible. 'The Lord your God is a devouring fire, a jealous God' (Deuteronomy 4.24). Yet the nature of God is pure love, light in whom there is no darkness at all (1 John 1.5). Once the outline, the glimmer of the iridescent pearl is seen in the mirror of the mind and its exquisite form hailed by the soul, it takes priority in the life of the person, as at once he is torn forcibly from unthinking conformity with the company with which he once identified himself. This was a childish response to the safety that is afforded by the weight of sheer numbers. These try to escape the realities of life by a thoughtless witness to vacuity that masquerades as purpose. Well does Jesus say, 'Do not store up for yourselves treasure on earth where it grows rusty and moth-eaten, and thieves break in to steal it. Store up treasure in heaven, where there is no moth and no rust to spoil it, no thieves to break in and steal. For where your treasure is, there will your heart be also' (Matthew 6.19-21). It is, however, the illusion of ownership and the comfortable safety that it engenders that seduces the multitudes. For most it remains an impossible ideal, but even the comparatively few who do acquire great wealth find that they are imprisoned by it to the extent of directing much of their attention to its preservation. If God were with them, they would be enabled instead to administer it to the benefit of their fellow creatures, knowing that abiding happiness is never individual and solitary but always shared and communal. The one who glimpses the light of God begins, at least vaguely, to see this reversal of the typical human hierarchy of priorities.

The bracing atmosphere of spiritual aspiration is therefore rather bleak, since the aspirant is now largely bereft of the throng that previously encompassed him and gave him an illusory protection by their sheer numbers. He is lifted up in order to see the kingdom of God, likened to the pearl of great price in Jesus' parable (Matthew 13.45-6). It is noteworthy that in this parable, as in the one immediately preceding it — concerning treasure being buried in a field — the person who has been given a glimpse of the entire treasure has to leave it behind until he can afford to buy it. He cannot simply proceed to appropriate it. In the same way, an experience of God's abiding love and the grace that flows out to embrace the happy person who has received it, is not meant to last long. After it comes the precipitate descent to the foothills of the spiritual life and the slow arduous ascent of the mountain of transfiguration where the treasure may be more thoroughly identified and claimed. Thus Moses, who met God as intimately as it is allowed mortal man to know the divine presence, was shown the plan of the temple, which is in fact the ideal society even more than a solitary edifice. Then he was told, 'See that you work to the design which you were shown on the mountain' (Exodus 25.40). It is poignant that in the end even he was not faultless enough to set foot on the Promised Land, but was allowed merely to see it at a distance from the peak of the mountain of Pisgah. Even today we have not actualized the divine plan of the ideal society in any part of the world, so few are the visionary lovers of God in the vast concourse of their unseeing neighbours. We cannnot claim the blessing until we are fully ready to receive it.

Thus the vision fades, and the darkness of contemporary life enfolds the aspirant once more as he descends to his place in the prosaic ranks of his fellows. If he is unwise enough to discuss the revelation with anyone else he is sure to be deflated. Some will indicate that he is mentally ill, or at least indisposed enough to need a complete break from his work. Others, more piously orientated, may think in terms of the devil, the creature clothed with the glittering light of counterfeit authority. All alike are secretly jealous even if unaware of their destructive intent. Well does Jesus say, 'Do not give dogs what is holy; do not throw your pearls to the pigs; they will only trample on them, and turn and tear you to pieces' (Matthew 7.6). The pearl is indeed a fragile commodity and has to be carefully guarded in the soul of the recipient. 'He who speaks does not know; he who knows does not speak', is the way Lao-Tsu expresses this great truth. It also exposes finely the difference between occult knowledge, or gnosis, and divine wisdom, which is all-encompassing and universally available to those ready to receive it. But it cannot be attained by any earthly riches; it is gained laboriously in the school of life itself with its manifold experiences; and no one experience is of less value than another, at least to the person who is awake, for all lead him further from his innate tendency to comfortable stagnation towards the goal of self-actualization in the form of Christ.

The intimation that comes to the typical man in the street can vary in intensity from a liberating illumination, such as altered the lives of Moses, when he saw the burning bush, or St Paul on the road to Damascus, or Jakob Boehme, when the burning light of God infused him in his own moment of contemplation, to an ineffable inner warmth of love that tells him that he does matter in a world of countless creatures, so many that God himself would seem hard-pressed to recognize them all. The current name for all this is the 'peak experience', and in recent years it has been the object of much study and description. Yet the more it is reified, made into an object to classify and control, the more does its delicate glow become diffused and subtly debased. The 'near-death experience' that is from time to time reported by those who were 'clinically dead', but who had been resuscitated just in time for complete brain function to be restored to normality, comes decidedly into this category. A new purpose for living has been shown to those whose mortal lives were at the point of extinction: spiritual priorities at last take precedence in what remains of their work on earth. All these experiences, from the most expansive and dramatic to the purely intimate still small voice of God in the soul, give the person some preview of eternal life. Something of its range is grasped by the soul in the space of an incredibly short period of time.

This is what we all seek, an asssurance of meaning that cannot be obtained by pure thought. The God of the philosophers is often a cold, distant being who has little direct contact with his creation. Theology, if it is to be dynamic and imperative, has to be infused with the warmth of the living God, the God of Abraham, Isaac and Jacob that Pascal met in his own dramatic illumination, perhaps not so very different from that experienced by St Thomas Aquinas at the end of his brilliant career of scholastic theology. But the vision kills — as it may have done the learned Dominican saint himself — in order to bring forth new life.

2 The Inner Directive

The fleeting vision that God gives us shows the way to a God-centred life, one modelled on the Word made flesh who lived among us, and revealed to us the glory of a fully actualized human being. The way, however, demands of us an absolute obedience to the spirit within us. The spirit is the highest function of the soul: through it God is known: that of God in every man, the indwelling Christ. This obedience is in turn a function of the conscience, which can be thought of as our inner awareness of the soul or true self. This contains within it the totality of moral values by which the aware, and therefore fully awakened, person directs his actions.

The conscience itself has grades of authority. It first shows itself, indeed appears to be inflicted, in childhood by our parents, and few of us completely outgrow the opinions and prejudices of our immediate family circle, no matter how emancipated we may believe ourselves to be as adults. But the parental influence, provided it is based on honest, moral principles, does serve to inculcate in us certain fundamental attitudes that are essential for harmonious relationships with those around us. In other words, the impress of our parents and teachers is an inevitable aspect of the process of learning whereby we all come to take our place in the world with its accepted standards and practices. If we diverge from what is expected of us we are punished, even ostracized. And so we reflect our parents', and later our teachers', views on many topics, profane and sacred alike. Where truth ends and pre-judice begins is an ill-defined terrain: perhaps truth is beyond our conception, even in later life, until humility endows us with a deeper understanding of moral values, a humility based on experience and fructified by love.

It is certain that the insensitive imposition of opinions on the child can easily quench the spirit for exploration and self-expression within, but provided the spirit is not crushed by the tyranny of an enforced, ill-assimilated uniformity, the endeavour of the soul to obey what is demanded of it from outside helps to develop the will and stimulates the awareness of the self.

> My son, do not think lightly of the Lord's discipline,
> nor lose heart when he corrects you;
> for the Lord disciplines those whom he loves;
> he lays the rod on every son whom he acknowledges.

In this passage (Hebrews 12.6, which finds its basis in Proverbs 3.11-12), we see an analogy between the firm discipline that a loving father lays upon his child with the love of God that is satisfied with nothing less than its creatures' perfection. The earthly father, unlike God, has his emotional limitations that flame forth as prejudices, but nevertheless the concern of the child's mentors easily outweighs their defects, provided, of course, they are well-intentioned and mentally balanced people. Our present permissive society shows, in its rejection of discipline, that the elementary conscience derived from those who should be our example is an important adjunct to the developing person. The current tendency to marital breakdown and one-parent families does not lead to the formation of a strong moral core in the offspring, who tend later to drift off into undesirable associations in order to compensate, albeit unconsciously, for the poor initial inner stability they inherited. If our attitudes are not formed around the object we should admire and love, other less worthy objects will take its place.

As the child attains adolescence so he is very likely to cast off all previously accepted religious and moral dogma. This is because the discipline set by these imposed ideas tends to be tedious and apparently irrelevant. Instead the young adult identifies himself with the spirit of the age which is incarnated in the opinions and life-styles of his peers. These may range from a socially radical stance that, at least intellectually, affects solidarity with and concern for the poor and downtrodden to a nihilistic dismissal of all responsibility that is all too common in those who become addicted to drugs. This way was epitomized in the first part of the Parable of the Prodigal Son. It seemed predestined that the thoughtless youth should jettison all family responsibility, spending his inheritance on worthless things until he touched bare penury. He could, in our present society, just as easily have sacrificed his will to discern, his ability to discriminate, to the leaders of a fashionable cult or to the subtle mind-obliterating enticements of an addictive drug. In the latter instance the conscience is completely obfuscated, whereas cult leaders infiltrate and pervert the inner seat of judgement by side-stepping its fundamental power of independent choice and subtly imposing upon it a pseudo-moral system of values directed to the benefit of those leaders.

Yet God is ultimately in control of all this mess; if not, there could be no hope of healing. I believe that it was the Holy Spirit that led the Prodigal Son away from the security of the parental home in somewhat the same way as he directed Abraham from the comfort of Mesopotamia to the unknown land of Canaan. Yet what a contrast! The latter is a story of God-directed dedication, the former, of pure hedonistic folly. But it was in both cases the Spirit of God that led them to their final abode, at once known from the beginning and yet unknown until entered upon in awe and trepidation. This is because our true abode is with God, whatever country we may inhabit.

In the course of a more orderly life, the youth has superimposed upon the training that he has received from home and school the *mores* of his peer group. This may be a professional class, a trade union or simply the opinions of those amongst whom he lives. Group loyalty can attain an overwhelming psychic pressure. A failure to conform may ultimately result in cruel exclusion from the support afforded by the group, a devastating ostracism. Jesus had to experience this at the end of his life, when he failed to fulfil the nationalistic expectations of his followers, who had hoped that he would have been the man to liberate Israel from Roman occupation. Indeed, the factors that led the people at large to follow Jesus must have been mixed and varied: his charismatic powers must have been the source of much of his attraction, but a few genuinely loved him with as much love as unredeemed man can muster. When he apparently failed, that love, like a frail candle flame, flickered precariously, and was almost but not quite extinguished. It is a hard thing to confront the shallowness of much public opinion, see its unconscious cruelty comfortably blanketed in pious hypocrisy, and consciously dissociate oneself from it. The courage to be oneself, no longer a mouthpiece of parental

11

conditioning or group loyalty, exceeds the power of description. As Christ said, 'Whoever cares for his own safety is lost, but if a man will let himself be lost for my sake and for the gospel, that man is safe' (Mark 8:35). But the faith needed for this renunciation is enormous, indeed beyond pure human strength. It requires the divine assistance, which comes to a person in his extremity. It is the juxtaposition of the divine and human wills.

The light within, if it is allowed to burn and illumine the way ahead, cuts out all diversions and unmercifully exposes all subterfuge. It is the vision of wholeness that cannot be evaded once it has been acknowledged. It is the vocation, the call to the spiritual life, that should inform all ordained religious groups in their submission to God, to their leaving self behind. And yet the self that is exposed is of much greater validity than anything renounced. It is the very seed of life in the soul; it is the spirit fully active and in direct contact with the Holy Spirit, not unconsciously but in willed service. In most people, however, the call is not so much to an exclusively spiritual profession as to a dedicated life of service in some secular field. Such a field may have obvious healing connotations like counselling or the healing ministry itself, but it can just as well be the unspectacular work the aspirant is performing in everyday life. Is the labour of an artisan of less value than that of a professional worker in such fields as medicine, law or finance? The answer lies in the person, not in the nature of the work, for all trades and professions have their own justification, inasmuch as each is in its own way vital to the community as a whole. How often has the prompt assistance of a humble labourer brought light to the troubled person whom he has met in the course of a day's work! How often does the cold, aloof attitude of the professional worker frighten or estrange those who have come to him for help! In not a few instances it is the specialist or expert who needs help as much as those who consult him.

It is not uncommon for a person to wonder whether he is doing God's will or whether he has not heard the divine voice and has failed to obey the call to a more spiritual kind of life that God had prepared for him. The answer is invariably this: be still and know the presence of God in the moment of doubt. The work that we have to do is what is at present within our compass. To please God it should be done efficiently and with concern for others; in other words, there should be a love of the work itself no less than for those whom the person is serving in that work. This is all that is required of us. If we prove ourselves worthy of this apparently minor task, God will show us the way to a more exalted spiritual work, according always to his will. In this respect the Parable of the Talents (Matthew 25.14-30) is especially relevant. The servant who worked profitably with a small sum of money was commended by his master, and as a reward, as well as due recognition for his trustworthiness and competence, was given an even larger responsibility. By contrast, the servant who was lazy and hid his master's money in a hole in the ground was roundly condemned. Even what he had was taken from him, and he was cast ignominiously out of the property. The parable also teaches us how important our period of incarnation is for our eternal destiny. We are expected to learn something from every circumstance of life, so that at the end we may emerge as wise, compassionate people. Our manifold experiences are here to make us respond with sensitivity to the problems and suffering of our fellow creatures. In this way we too may emerge as profitable servants, fit for the kingdom of God in the life eternal. It is a strange thought that the talents with which we are entrusted include the painful stripping experiences of the past. These, far from being disastrous, are the very basis of the work ahead of us when we have attained sufficient balance to accept them and use them constructively.

The intimation, then, of God's light in the soul leads to a radical reappraisal of the person's conscience. To be sure its basic lineaments — honesty, charity, courtesy, loyalty and a warm compassion towards all living creatures — remain unchanged. It is the approach to these great moral virtues that is reconsidered. The loyalty now transcends family or group pressures, the honesty goes beyond a merely formal lip-service to various ideals, even those connected with traditional religious observance, to an investigation of the entire edifice of truth as is apparent to the person's inner discernment. The essential theme is awareness; the intimation of God's presence serves to awaken the sleeping one not merely to the divine invitation to enter into a new life, but also to the responsibilities inherent in his present situation. The present reality and the future promise are superimposed to illumine the moment in hand: time is shown as a vital part to the overall scheme of salvation to prepare the creature for the knowledge of eternity. Where the fully aware mind touches the things of everyday life it also touches eternal nature, the mystical form out of which all phenomena emerge. This awareness is not simply a down-to-earth, essentially practical application of common sense, vital as this is for our life day by day. It is also an awareness of the divine providence that sustains the world, the love that moves the sun and the other stars about which Dante writes in *The Divine Comedy* in respect of his great vision of paradise. Then at last our daily toil, frustrated as it so often is with worry and apparent failure, takes on a completely new perspective. It is our mounting of a small step on the ladder of perfection. The inner attitude is the important gauge of success rather than the outer achievement. The diminishing years of ageing thus present a greater challenge than do the satisfying achievements of youth: how do we respond to outer impoverishment, to the anonymity of retirement, the impotence of senescence? Do we emanate frustration or serenity, resentment or peace? When the crowds derided Jesus on the cross, he called out to his Father to forgive them for they did not know what they were doing. When Jonah accused God of back-pedalling in not destroying the Ninevites, he was told by God, 'Should I not be sorry for the great city of Nineveh, with its hundred and twenty thousand who cannot tell their right hand from their left, and cattle without number?' (Jonah 4.11). This figuratively bovine stupidity of the people of Nineveh is the type of all purely worldly awareness. They are blind, not because they have no eyes, but because they are too witless to open them and start to see the true life.

The sixth chapter of the Book of Isaiah has much to tell us: first there is the wonderful account of the prophet's vision of God in the temple and of his awareness of his own and the national uncleanness, the purging of his personal unworthiness, and his commission to serve the Lord unconditionally. He says, 'Here I am, send me'. Then God says to him concerning the people, 'You may listen and listen, but you will not understand. You may look and look again, but you will never know. This people's wits are dulled, their ears are deafened and their eyes blinded, so that they cannot see with their eyes nor listen with their ears nor understand with their wits, so that they may turn and be healed.' When Isaiah asks how long this sad state of affairs is to last, God indicates that a terrible destruction has first to take place before any true repentance may occur. The people in fact gaze at trivialities as their attention is seduced by falsehood. Their hearing is diverted into unprofitable fields of frivolity, in order to escape the voice of the living God. 'Hear, O Israel: the Lord our God is the only Lord' (Deuteronomy 6.4), the watchword of Judaism, is quoted directly by Jesus in his definition of the greatest commandment of loving God with heart, soul, mind and strength (Mark 12.29-30). The text in Isaiah, quoted on several occasions in the New Testament, almost sounds as if God had deliberately perverted the awareness of the people in much the same way as he was said to have hardened Pharaoh's heart against granting Moses' requests. In fact, it is much more probable that he had foreseen the stubborn intransigence of the people (and Pharaoh) and had made contingency plans accordingly. The ultimate plan was the incarnation of Christ himself, whose ministry had at least helped some to move beyond the death of the physical body to the eternal life of the Spirit. But even today the blindness and deafness to truth is still widespread among most people including some who believe they are following the spiritual path.

The period of Advent that finds its completion in Christmas reminds us especially that now is the time. We have to awaken now to be in attendance on our Lord, whose coming is eternally near and yet cannot be defined on any temporal scale. Lest we should be lost in the frivolity of the heedless world or trapped in improvident folly, like the Foolish Virgins who neglected to bring oil with them to fill their lamps, we are admonished to be prepared at all times for the great moment, which is in fact every moment, the intersection of time and eternity. The intimation of God's presence and his unceasing providence in the course of our lives is our Advent call; we have to stay awake to welcome the Lord into our lives. He knocks at the door of the soul and patiently awaits our invitation to enter. Usually we are deaf to his courteous knock, but once the intimation of his radiance has penetrated our obtuse sensitivity, we become more alert to his presence and more prompt in our response. As we reflect on our past, so we begin to see the inadequacy of our previous style of life. The tenor of our deeper inner responses, as well as our immediate conduct, to the various contingencies that punctuate daily life, is a measure of the development of the conscience in power and authority. What was a mere repository of attitudes assimilated from the outside world and inherited from our parents is becoming fashioned into a well-contoured conscience of independent stature. The conscience in this way becomes the mirror in which we see our behaviour reflected to ourselves moment by moment in life's unending show. The impingent ray on that sensitive mirror modifies our subsequent response and the conduct that follows from it; and so we are able to cope with life's crises in a constructive, adult way, being of increasing use to our neighbour, who is in fact the whole created order, when we are fully alive to the moment upon us.

The conscience so purified and strengthened becomes our inner lantern. By it we can proceed forward to the place of truth. No longer need we be attracted by the promise of worldly rewards, for a greater prize is distantly in view. The pearl of great price far outstrips the finest treasure that the world has to offer, for it alone points to a life of meaning, whose end is the raising up of the whole creation from death to immortality. If we think again about the Wise and Foolish Virgins with their lamps prepared to escort their Lord into the wedding chamber, the oil can be equated with their preliminary discipline in prayer and daily work. The alert ones are available to greet the bridegroom, whereas their sluggish companions have no spiritual resources on which to call in a time of emergency. When we are put to the test, it is the inner life that alone can sustain us. If, like so many people, we have virtually no inner resources to strengthen us, we will be overcome by the magnitude of the present demand. But when God is near us, we can call upon him in confidence, and his Spirit will support us.

> But now this is the word of the Lord,
> the word of your creator, O Jacob,
>   of him who fashioned you, Israel:
> Have no fear; for I have paid your ransom;
> I have called you by my name and you are my own
> (Isaiah 43.1).

As the conscience becomes more acute in response, so does the presence of God become clearer to the person. He shines in the 'new man' that is emerging from the shell of a past life like the chrysalis of a caterpillar out of which the radiant butterfly bursts forth.

The conditioning that we received in childhood, provided it was based on integrity and administered with concern, is reinforced as we grow into our own identity. But what had initially to be imposed on us for our own good now becomes the foundation of an edifice of our unique construction. On the other hand, what was prejudiced and spiritually unsure is cut away, so that the truth can be revealed and sustained. This is the truth that sets us free to be ourselves, enslaved neither to another person nor to any alien ideology. These tend to insinuate themselves as a way of release, but their end is subtle bondage. The truth of God alone brings us the liberty to be ourselves and to grow into authentic persons.

3   The Shadow Antagonist

It is one thing to possess an adult conscience of mature contour; it is something else to act in the world in accordance with that inner directive. Our divided consciousness, at least with regard to ethical matters, is notorious: St Paul laments his own moral dilemma in his celebrated words: 'We know that the law is spiritual; but I am not; I am unspiritual, the purchased slave of sin. I do not even acknowledge my own actions as mine for what I do is not what I want to do, but what I detest.' He continues that the good he wants to do, he fails to do, but what he does is the wrong which is against his will. He discovers the principle that when he wants to do the right, only the wrong is within his reach. In his inmost self he delights in the law of God, but he perceives that there is a different law in his bodily members which fights against the law approved of by his reason. He is made a prisoner under the law that is in his members, the law of sin. This extended passage, from Romans 7.14-25, reaches the conclusion that the human will to do good is impotent except in the strength of God in Christ. And so the acute conscience is being subtly undermined by impulses deep in the unconscious, shadow powers that betray the divine image in which we were all created.

In psychodynamic theory the shadow is seen as the dark unconscious element that is opposed to the active, conscious will to good that should guide the civilized person. It is subtly destructive of all good intentions, and emerges in conscious life as a tendency to self-aggrandisement that acts with stealthy determination to undermine all that stands in the way of one's own schemes of advancement and power. If this aspect of the personality is evaded, repressed or consciously denied, it attains frightening momentum and can invade and overwhelm the conscious life of the person. Not infrequently it is projected on to some other person, who acts as a convenient scapegoat. This projection is typically unconscious, and is the basis of much racism, religious intolerance and xenophobia. What we

18

find intolerable in ourselves is most conveniently jettisoned upon those for whom we harbour an innate suspicion. In this irrational way, using a circular argument, we can actually justify our antipathy, at least to our own deluded minds.

But the shadow side of our psyche also has a more constructive component: it gives an earthy roundness to the personality, which without it would tend to radiate an insipid goodness devoid of effective driving power. It is the energizing focus of the personality, without which no creative good would emerge. If one part of a person's life is service to those around him, the other part directs service to himself. Without elementary concern for our own welfare we would soon be submerged by the voracious tide of life. Enlightened self-concern must therefore take immediate precedence over our concern for our neighbour's welfare. Only when we are strong in our inner psychic life can we proceed with some safety to serve others who are in need. The demands of the insensitive mass of humanity can drain the servant of God to the core. By prayer alone can he be restored in a time of emergency. It is, however, the shadow side that takes a more longterm care of the servant, and it will not permit any further draining of inner healing resources. The spiritual life does not so much move beyond personal demands as work towards their integration and ultimate transmutation in an existence that is no longer selfish but dedicated instead to the care of all created things. We should, on the one hand, beware of a tendency towards self-indulgent idleness that satisfies the individual at the expense of the greater community. But the opposite extreme, of becoming a doormat over which the feet of the ungracious masses trample, is equally to be avoided. Apart from its obviously destructive effect on the mind and body of the one who serves, it may also result quite subtly in making him into something of a martyr, at least in his own eyes. Darkness is at its most dangerous when it assumes some of the qualities of light: righteous indignation in the name of religious propriety against deviant groups, leading to their persecution and destruction, is another good example of the same invidious tendency. How then do we distinguish between the light of God that burns away all illusion as a consuming fire and the false light of the shadow consciousness that may seduce the very elect? The uncreated energies of the Deity by which we know of his presence (since no man can see God directly and remain alive) blind us momentarily, as they did St Paul in his Damascus-road experience. Even if our physical sight is not obscured, then at least our normal consciousness with its overtones of complacency and comfortable compliance with the status quo is overwhelmed, as we confront our unworthiness in the light of truth. The call to ministry of the prophets of Israel, especially that of Isaiah, demonstrates this quite clearly; and then we are accepted in a love that raises us to a very different vision of service as a new life opens up to us.

By contrast, the arresting glitter of the shadow consciousness exalts us, promising us great things provided we obey its instructions. The story of the seduction of Eve by the serpent (in Genesis 3) is the archetypal example: the human is initiated into the tantalizing mysteries of life, as he illicitly partakes of the fruit of the tree of the knowledge of good and evil. He may be master of the world, but there is no love, which comes of God alone, and all his endeavours end on a mute note of failure, death and oblivion. The temptation of the Fall is repeated in the life of Christ after his baptism and the downflow of the Holy Spirit upon him. But now we have a man full of the love of God who does not need displays of power, whether psychical or political, to substantiate the authority of his perfect humanity. Where there is love there is no need of anything else. But what is love? It is at the very centre of the pearl of great price. The word is used incessantly, promiscuously in fact. But until its chastity is shown, we cannot know a proper human being.

To return to the dichotomy of human nature described and lamented so tirelessly by St Paul, we have a person with his head in the clouds of glory, with Moses on Mount Sinai in the presence of the Deity, and his feet on the soggy earth of desire, lust and gluttony, indeed the wilderness around the sacred mountain. When Moses descends with the tablets of the sacred law, he finds the people worshipping a golden calf fashioned by his brother Aaron, who one might hope would have known better, since he was the mouthpiece of Moses during the time of his interviewing Pharaoh with an eye to the release of his subect brethren. The entire sacred history of the remainder of the Old Testament is an account of the gradual purification of the Jews working towards an elevation of the bodily passions in the supreme service of love to both God and man. And then to the Jews comes the supreme privilege of forming the physical body from which Jesus is fashioned, one in whom there is a perfect union of the human and divine natures. But even his example and the grace that follows his supreme sacrifice can only gradually be assimilated by his disciples and those who follow in the way throughout the subsequent centuries. The giving up of all one has in order to acquire the costly pearl is hard, especially as there is no certainty, in one's more sober moments, that either the pearl exists as an objective reality or that it can in any case be acquired. Perhaps it too was a mere will-o'-the-wisp that led one to an impossible task, an illusion that sprang out of one's psychological inadequacy in the hard cut and thrust of the world of solid reality. And we do not know! Nor can we know except by travelling on an unknown, yet well-charted, path.

The way forward is by faith, a faith that the noble outweighs the ignoble, that honesty is preferable to deceit, that service to others is finer than mere proprietorship, that death is, in its many guises, not the end but rather the gateway to a fuller life, whether here on earth (for the one who still lives in the body) or in the larger world beyond our mortal vision. But we can say with Peter, after many would-be disciples left Jesus because of his apparently outrageous teaching, 'Lord, to whom shall we go? Your words are words of eternal life. We have faith, and we know that you are the Holy One of God' (John 6.68-69). One can meditate sadly on Peter's ambivalent faith when it was severely taxed, but he did persist in the face of his humiliation and press onwards to a real sanctity.

Did Jesus in fact know of the shadow consciousness, or was he so absolutely spotless that no mortal temptation could resonate within him? Traditional piety would flinch with horror at any such suggestion, but if Jesus was truly fully human, it would be imperative that he should bear the full impact of human passion. This is the inner meaning of the Incarnation. It may have been that as a youth he was so raised above everyday, material things as to be uncontaminated by even their atmosphere, but when his adult ministry began, he accepted a baptism of repentance administered by John in the wilderness. It is interesting that in Matthew's account of the proceedings,

John demurs from administering such a baptism to Jesus, declaring that he rather should receive baptism at the hands of Jesus. However, Jesus replies, 'Let it be so for the present; we do well to conform in this way with all that God requires' (Matthew 3.13-15). Immediately after the baptism the Holy Spirit descends like a dove to alight upon him, and a voice from heaven acclaims him as his Son, his Beloved on whom his favour rests.

Thereupon Jesus is led into the wilderness by the Holy Spirit to be tempted by the devil. Then in no uncertain way the shadow consciousness descends on Jesus also, more like an enveloping fog than a dove, and it too, like the Holy Spirit, remains with him until his death. Did he respond negatively to this massive incubus, assumed as part of the healing of the world? We remember how the woman, who had suffered from haemorrhages (probably from the womb) for twelve years, drained him when she touched him without permission. We recall his irritation with the disciples at their obtuseness in understanding the nature of his mission, and with his own family, when they tried to insinuate themselves and claim special priority in the course of his teaching work. The Syro-Phoenician woman also evoked his irritation when she sought healing for her daughter, who was not Jewish. 'It is not right to take the children's bread and throw it to the dogs' (Matthew 15.21-28). He submits in the end but only as a concession to the woman's extreme faith coupled with her humility. All this is very human. Many involved in the healing ministry know how the influx of unceasing demands can provoke increasing agitation, until one is forced to shut down completely for the preservation of one's basic sanity. Jesus was also capable of considerable anger when confronted by hypocrisy, especially the type of religious casuistry that could cheat the underdog. The powerful denunciations of Matthew 23 bear full weight to this assertion.

We remember the words of Hebrews 5.7-10,

> In the days of his earthly life he offered up prayers and petitions, with loud cries and tears, to God who was able to deliver him from the grave. Because of his humble submission his prayer was heard: son though he was, he learned obedience in the school of suffering and, once perfected, became the source of eternal salvation for all who obey him, named by God high priest in the succession of Melchizedek.

The perfection alluded to may have been a complete acceptance of the darkness around him, no longer provoking his irritation, agitation or anger, but instead consummated in patience, forebearing and forgiveness. These sublime attributes are especially in evidence during the painful humiliation of his passion ending with his death on the cross between two criminals. But this final acceptance and forgiveness is of a different order to a spineless, permissive goodwill that is in fact far removed from the actual facts of earthly life. In other words, Jesus preached personal resurrection, not mere spiritual uplift, and in his ministry he effected something of this rising from the dead in all who were open to him.

We, in imitation of our Lord, also enter the shadow realms after we have committed our lives to his service. Spiritual initiation is succeeded by a descent into the personal shadow area. This is both a test of our dedication to God and a commencement of the vital work of raising up our inner sickness to God for healing. Furthermore, our own psychic darkness is in, as it were, creative tension with that of all other people, since we are all members of the one body. Therefore our individual healing is a presage, indeed a very start, of the healing of the beloved community whose end is the renewal of the entire creation. The yearning for wholeness that we all, no matter how inarticulately, share cannot come about until the sickness is fully exposed with nothing hidden in the darkness. It is written of Adam and Eve that they lived in complete openness to each other and to God in paradise. After the Fall they could no longer face God directly because they knew they were unwholesome. Nor could they face each other with that unself-conscious, child-like trust of paradise any longer because their very sexuality had become strangely polluted. In the same way we bear the impact of that sinfulness whose consequence is to sully all personal relationships, where love has been degraded to physical lust and trust to opportunistic compliance. When Christ was nailed to the cross his naked sexuality was once more made visible to the onlookers, as is indeed our own when we are shortly to die. At last we have nothing to hide as all our most intimate secrets are laid bare for all the world to see. And then we make the shattering discovery that our secrets are held in common with all mankind. But we long for the time when this common inheritance may be shared in the noonday warmth of life and with the innocence that marked the mutual regard of our allegorical ancestors Adam and Eve before they fell from grace. Then at last the shadow will have been embraced in the light of God's love, and healing will be complete.

Meanwhile the way to perfection includes a descent to our own private hell in which all the debris of unrequited passion lies exposed, accepted, and placed on the altar of dedication in the assurance of divine healing. These objects of revulsion are held in common by all mankind, but when even one person can move spiritually towards accepting them in love, somehow the burden they exert on us all is significantly lightened. T. S. Eliot wrote well of the situation in his poem *The Hollow Men*:

> Between the idea
> And the reality
> Between the motion
> And the act
> Falls the Shadow.

As St Paul says, there is something that always seems to thwart our best intentions, our noblest ideals. It corrupts the decency within us, like the filth inside the cup that spoils the contents, no matter how industriously the rim is cleaned. What lies inside festers until it has been drained as an abscess. The process is always painful, but the relief that follows its completion is so profound that it seems to annul all the previous suffering. The vocation of the Suffering Servant is now fulfilled in the individual life of the believer, 'The chastisement he bore is health for us and by his scourging we are healed' (Isaiah 53.5). What he has experienced personally now has to be given to his fellows. In so doing he not only assists others but also grows progressively in spiritual strength with its concomitant authority.

The most superficially placed flaws are obvious enough: uncontrollable sexual desire and a covetousness that drives its victim to crime, even murder. Thus the two most significant encounters in the Bible of evil within the depths of the psyche concern David and Ahab. The former, a valiant warrior, well informed by the Spirit of God and generously endowed with

wives and concubines, nevertheless stoops to sordid adultery
with Bathsheba, the wife of Uriah the Hittite, a faithful soldier in
David's army. David conspires to have Uriah slain in battle,
after which sin he takes Bathsheba as his wife. All seems well on
the surface, but underneath there is a stinking cesspit of
murder. And so God sends Nathan the prophet to tell David a
parable of a rich man who appropriates the solitary beloved
ewe-lamb of a poor man to serve a passing traveller while he
keeps his own larger flock intact. When David denounces the
rich man for his ruthlessness, Nathan utters the fateful words,
'You are the man' (2 Samuel 12.1-7). The great warrior has been
exposed in his naked lust that has not shrunk from killing
another man, better than he himself. Although David confesses
his sin and Nathan pronounces God's qualified forgiveness,
terrible internecine strife ravages the royal family. It culminates
in the insurrection and death of David's favourite son Absalom.
How often has this drama of family disintegration been enacted,
albeit much less violently, in the course of many instances of
adultery!

In the case of Ahab who covets the vineyard of Naboth, it is
his evil wife Jezebel who conspires to have Naboth condemned
to death when he remains adamant in his determination not to
yield his property to the king. But as Ahab proceeds to take
possession of the unjustly appropriated land, Elijah the prophet
confronts the king to his face and denounces him without
mitigation (1 Kings 21). The stark theme in both these cases of
wickedness is, 'You are the man'. In one way or another we all
seem destined to experience a similar confrontation. It may
range from a treacherous betrayal of a friend or colleague, which
has been exposed to our shame, to a humiliating brush with the
law in respect of a penal offence. We may try to wriggle our way
out of the ensuing mess so as to save our face, but both we and
those involved in the matter know of the emptiness of our
defence, that, like the emperor in Hans Christian Andersen's
story, we have no clothes on even if we act as if arrayed in fine
apparel. These acts of betrayal, lust and dishonesty are so much
part of the human condition that none of us can escape their
impact.

In what is probably the most enigmatic of the parables, that of
the Dishonest Steward (Luke 16.1-9), Jesus actually appears to

advise us to use our worldly wealth to win friends for ourselves. In the Authorized Version of the Bible, worldly wealth is translated much more tellingly as 'the mammon of unrighteousness', reminding us that money passes through many hands, most of which are not especially clean, either physically or morally. Yet almost immediately after the parable we are told that no servant can be the slave of two masters because of the divided loyalty that is involved: we cannot serve God and money (Luke 16.13). The reconciliation of these two apparently contradictory teachings of Jesus seems to be related to the maturing of spiritual awareness. The unjust steward is actually commended for his astuteness in getting rapid part-payments from his master's debtors, an action of pure self-interest, inasmuch as he may gain supporters after his likely dismissal from his present employment. It would seem that his master is not only a man of the world who can appreciate his servant's adroitness in saving his own skin as well as getting as much as possible for his employer under difficult circumstances, but also a person blessed with a fine sense of humour. This is also a picture of God and his relationship with us: he accepts our frailty with a gentle humour and is always ready to forgive us. We may hope that, after his narrow escape consequent on the humanity of his master, the steward would deal far more responsibly in the future with the things of this world. He might eventually learn to treat money as a thing of God, to be used to the benefit of the community and not simply for his own ends. If all of us, to reflect on another of Jesus' sayings, were to pay to the worldly power what was its due, and to God what was his due (Mark 12.13-17), even the world's due would be lifted up to God, and the world itself moved onwards, ever so slightly it is true, to its ultimate state of resurrection.

Life, in other words, is seldom a straightforward affair. Its shadow region enmeshes us all in shady undertakings and moral ambiguity. Even if our own lives are genuinely pure, we cannot avoid rubbing up against corruption, vice and violence, in view of the murky background of money itself — often dishonestly acquired and used for very controversial purposes — and the moral disorder of those who handle it. As we enter the service of God, so we have to descend into the pit, not so very different in essence from the lions' pit into which

Daniel was hurled after he had refused to pray to king Darius (Daniel 6). But just as Daniel was preserved, in that fine story, from the ferocity of the lions, so are we also protected as long as we put our trust in God and never take our eyes off the present moment. This was the secret of Jesus' inviolability in the face of all the world's temptation and stain. But he was shielded from nothing. Far from it, his sensitivity accentuated his great vulnerability both in the period of triumph and during the barely penetrable gloom of Gethsemane and Calvary.

4 The Cloud and the Fire

In the course of the Israelites' exodus, the presence of God never left the people. It had a tangible form:

> They set out from Succoth and encamped at Etham on the edge of the wilderness. And all the time the Lord went before them, by day a pillar of cloud to guide them on their journey, by night a pillar of fire to give them light so that they could travel night and day. The pillar of cloud never left its place in front of the people by day, nor the pillar of fire by night (Exodus 13.20-2).

The physical presence of the Lord was intimately involved with his people during the whole period of their journey (Exodus 40.38). The fire did not so much replace the cloud as burn within it. In much the same way the divine presence never leaves us on our spiritual journey, whose destination is blazed forth by the radiance of the pearl of great price; we momentarily glimpsed it in a blessed state of illumination, after which we consecrated our very life to obtain it for our own. The cloud reminds us of the unknowable quality of God as we move on our daily routine in the world. Furthermore, the divine fire is stiflingly dulled by the thoughtless, unheeding, seething masses. And so our exodus from the world of selfish endeavour is attended by the cloud of unknowing into whose mysterious depths we commit ourselves in faith as we progress to the Promised Land of our own destiny. In the dense cloud the contours of the illuminated world are, paradoxically, more visible than in even the full glare of earthly wisdom. The initial illumination that led us on the quest of spiritual truth is now no longer a fleeting memory of the past; the memory is rather assuming a dominant part of our living awareness. In the cloud we see dim images of the light, images that draw us on further to the accomplishment of our great undertaking.

Yet in our everyday life we so often betray the call to full integrity which is the inner image of the pearl. The way upwards is also the way downwards, and the constant tensions of our present situation all too frequently lead us into attitudes and actions that shame us. One would have thought that we at least, striving for the good life, would not fail so miserably time after time. It is indeed the shadow consciousness striking back at us and with a vengeance. Is there any good in us at all, or are all our strivings mere gestures of egoistical concern for our reputation in this world and our preservation in the life of the world to come, always assuming, in our moments of dark agnosticism, that there is such a place of survival of the dead? All our lives are a journey to the grave: the hour that gives us independent life also takes it away from us as we move steadily and inexorably towards our common destination. When we betray our own inner ideals and are shown up as shallow frauds and hypocrites, we put ourselves out of communion with our peers. The common march goes on without us as we sit despondently on the wayside, ignored by the passing parade. So, of course, did the Prodigal Son, but in the depth of his loneliness he met someone of whose presence he had been previously oblivious.

In other words, at times we are out of alignment with our fellows because of our own stupidity or wickedness, but as soon as we come to terms with our situation and do not try to extricate ourselves by our own manipulation, the divine presence will make itself known to us. It was, of course, always there, but before our debacle we were not available to receive it. When human solidarity is withdrawn from us we may, if we have courage and forebearance, be able to experience divine acceptance and help. It is a common spiritual insight that God loves us, irrespective of our worthiness. But unfortunately this insight remains remote from most people in the turmoil of their own lives, especially when they are sick, bereaved or unemployed. No one can convince another of his intrinsic worth, or that he has been forgiven his many sins; formal absolution itself may not completely still the inner qualms of regret. We have great difficulty in forgiving ourselves when we are strongly orientated in a moral dimension, so deep is the thrust of a stern, nagging conscience. This fact, incidentally, reminds us of the tyranny of an unyielding conscience, no matter how independent it is of past conditioning. If we cannot forgive ourselves, who then can convince us that we are forgiven?

If our attitudes and intentions are sincerely directed to what is morally right, the ultimate forgiver of sin, God himself, will tell us that all is well. And so we are read,

> My children, love must not be a matter of words or talk; it must be genuine, and show itself in action. This is how we may know that we belong to the realm of truth, and convince ourselves in his sight that even if our conscience condemns us, God is greater than our conscience, and knows all (1 John 3.18-20).

The passage goes on to say that if our conscience does not condemn us, then we can approach God with confidence. It follows therefore that God both reassures the sincere, but uncertain, conscience and then enables us to approach him in confident joy; thus the conscience itself grows in depth, as its tolerance broadens to accept much, both in the person himself and in his fellows, that would previously have been the occasion of revulsion, a rejection based essentially on the fear of contamination. It is a moment of great liberation when we no longer have to hold doggedly on to any spiritual principle externally inculcated, inasmuch as that principle is now so completely part of ourself that we accept it and venture out into new fields of experience. Thus Jeremiah prophesied the time when the Law would no longer have to be taught and obeyed as an outer ordinance, but would rather be an inviolable presence in the soul of the believer.

Two occasions in my own life bear out the fact of God's grace at times of personal crisis. Both occurred a long time ago, and their fruits can be surveyed with the detachment and tranquillity that the passing years bestow. On the first occasion I, in a fit of childish pique, put myself at variance with some colleagues who demanded work of me that seemed unfair, for the time was a major public holiday. My refusal to co-operate led to their cold-shouldering me; the ostracism was unbearable, for I would not concede their point of view. In desperation I drove out into the countryside, during which time a sudden peace descended on me. It also filled me with the resolution to make my peace with the others; when I had done this, heavenly accord flowed among us all. In that brief period in the wilderness, I had known the acceptance of God, and his peace had filled me with something infinitely more precious than the good opinions of people. I had been lifted to a higher level of reality, one that far outdistanced the narrow limits of the work in which I was routinely engaged, without in any way denigrating the importance of that work. Looking back on this episode, I can see that neither I nor the others were without blame, because the decision to do the work over the holiday period had been taken without my prior consultation. I have no doubt that I would have agreed wholeheartedly, had I first been consulted, but to have been ignored was more than my self-esteem could stand. When, however, I was infused with the peace of God, the usual sequence of apology, justification and recrimination simply dissolved away. I, in some measure, retained the memory of that peace, and it has remained an invaluable support through the vicissitudes of my subsequent life.

The other event that was to have a lasting effect on my spiritual development was centred on a minor motoring offence that I had committed. When the summons arrived, I was filled with terrible foreboding. I had never appeared in court before, and the possible punishment in store for me magnified itself to a gaol sentence in my fevered, innocent imagination. No doubt I would have been less overwhelmed with fruitless anxiety had there been someone else available with whom to discuss the matter, but living alone can impose an almost unbearable tension on a rigid, inexperienced conscience. Then suddenly I was aware of a presence of wordless strength behind me. It infused me with a power of love that had undertones of strength and direction, telling me (in wordless communication) not to be anxious and to do what was necessary to come to terms with the situation and put myself in right footing with the law. My whole personality seemed, at least subjectively, to have been not merely renewed but actually transfigured. Love, joy and peace flowed from me as I conducted a counselling session that afternoon in the squalid premises I then occupied, and I was guided along effortlessly to the appearance in court where the statutory punishment was pronounced: a nominal fine and a temporary endorsement of my driving licence. Even the publicity that I feared did not seem to materialize. What, however, I gained spiritually from that encounter with the law was out of all proportion to the anxiety and embarrassment I had suffered. The actual presence behind me during the spiritual encounter was so circumscribed and directive that I have often wondered whether it was my guardian angel, but for those of us who cannot accept such a metaphysical concept, it is enough to say that my 'higher self', or spirit, was in command of the situation. This spirit is in direct communion with the Holy Spirit of God. Once again the experience made an indelible impression on my mind, and was a crucial event in my developing spiritual awareness.

In these two experiences I was in a cloud of my own making. Had I been less childish in the first, and more careful and considerate in the second, I would never have known the darkness, but at a crucial moment I had yielded to innate impulses that, theoretically at least, should have been laid aside when I reached adult stature. But emotional maturity develops slowly and is probably never advanced in any earthly life. The emotionally mature person is in control of his feelings, whether of anger, fear or resentment, so that he neither lays their burden on other people nor is overwhelmed by them in a situation of crisis. Such a person can absorb the emotional disturbances of those around him and is in his own being a fine counsellor and also a minister of healing. We cannot either counsel or heal others effectively, until our own inner disturbances are not only faced but also integrated into our personalities. My two dramatic encounters with inner darkness brought me also to a knowledge of God that had previously been outside my experience. The pillar of cloud that seemed to judge my failings revealed its fire, a fire of purification and healing, when I was ready to accept its verdict, forgiveness and healing.

God is both in the little cloud, which we emanate in our baser moments and in the great cloud of unknowing, which we have to penetrate in trust if we are to know him. In the immortal words of *The Cloud of Unknowing*, 'By love may he be gotten and holden, but by thought never'. In our extremity, typified by that of the Prodigal Son, we are open to his love, which, like all genuine love, is unceasing, undemanding and universal. That love kindles the flame of love in our own hearts, and then a new dimension of living unfolds. Love is undemanding, inasmuch as it is not conditional on any prior worthiness on the part of the beloved, but the effect of that love sets extreme demands on the beloved, who then is enjoined to give love to all the world. In other words, the unconditional love of God brings with it a call to service so that all other creatures may also know that love, mediated by the particular person who has received the divine love. God's love operates through our own particular personalities, each of which is of unique value no matter how unprepossessing we may appear in the world. It not infrequently happens that an apparently insignificant person is an especially fine mediator of love, inasmuch as he is less concerned about himself and the image that he displays in the world around himself.

We read in 1 John 1.5 that God is light and in him there is no darkness at all. The cloud that he shows us is described aptly, though paradoxically, by mystics as 'dazzling darkness'. It is something of the smoke that filled the sanctuary while the threshold of the temple shook to its foundations, as the angelic host proclaimed the terrible holiness and glory of God in the tremendous vision of Isaiah, a vision that inaugurated his prophetic ministry. The cloud shows us the enormous gulf between us and a knowledge of God. Indeed, no one can see God directly and remain alive, so destructive are the uncreated energies that proceed from him, in the same way that our mortal sight would be irrevocably destroyed were we to gaze directly at the sun. As a person grows in spiritual authority, so he can come to God more directly and see the magnitude of his own unworthiness as well as the greater span of the divine acceptance.

The darkness can also be the result of our own poor sight. Just as the blind man cannot see his surroundings, so the majority of people are still spiritually blind, as we remember from the passage of Isaiah, quoted earlier, that follows the prophet's vision of God in the temple (Isaiah 6). Even the traveller on the spiritual path may experience periods of poor sight, as did Jesus momentarily on the cross when his Father's presence was so inapparent that he believed he had been forsaken by him. He had, during the period of his passion, to assume the full burden of human impotence and woe; without the experience of spiritual darkness that so often clouds the lives of the most devout believers no less than their indifferent fellows, he could not have spoken to the total human condition. The darkness sometimes takes on the quality of a failure of nerve or a destructive scepticism that obliterates all previously held belief, so that the aspirant flounders in a dark sea of meaninglessness tinged with dread.

To some believers all this is attributed to a malicious assault by the supramundane powers of darkness. It would, in any case, be futile to speculate too expansively about the origin of the impediments that block the spiritual path. Since we are all parts of the one body, it is not unreasonable to conjecture that a demonic influence could find its entry into the individual personality through some defect in it, the Achilles heel that we all have. It may be greed, covetousness, rancour or lust, to name only four common human failings. Few of us are immune in any of these aspects; indeed, their acknowledgement is part of our spiritual development. If they are accepted and then laid on God's altar in faith, they will be progressively constrained and ultimately healed and spiritualized. Thus greed can be transfigured to a yearning that all people may be fed; covetousness to the desire that all may be satisfied. The power of rancour may become a creative anger at the manifold injustices in the world which in turn is actualized in a fight against cruelty. Lust, an accentuation of the most powerful of all the human drives, intimately involved as it is with procreation, can be raised up to the level of love, which in turn helps the spiritualization of the other failings.

It is noteworthy that in the story of Job, the hero is tested quite deliberately by Satan under the aegis of God, his father no less than the father of Job. God will not countenance Job's death, but connives at all the other sufferings laid upon him. One always remembers the Old Testament affirmation of the unity and sovereignty of God in all his creation: 'I am the Lord, there is no other; I make the light, I create darkness, author alike of prosperity and trouble. I, the Lord, do all these things' (Isaiah 45.7). All this stands apparently in stark contrast to the Johannine doctrine, previously noted, of God being light without darkness (1 John 1.5). It seems probable that the darkness of creation is a secondary phenomenon related to the independent selfish use of free will by God's rational creatures. The legend has it that Lucifer, the prince of darkness, was originally the bearer of light in the angelic hierarchy, who overreached himself in trying to vie with his Creator. And now his light has been corrupted to darkness, as it misleads unwitting humans down the seductive path of self-aggrandisement to destruction. But fortunately, to return to Isaiah once more, God is in ultimate control: no phenomenon or event is outside his power and compassion. He created Lucifer in the same way that he created the monsters of cruelty in the world's long history. These perverted the power of life within them, just as the world's saints have glorified that life. Most of us lie uneasily some way between these two extremes; the spirit is indeed willing, but the flesh with its various failings is tragically weak; and the pearl cannot be acquired apart from either spirit or flesh.

One always hopes for the conversion (which means a turning to the light) and healing of all deviant creatures, whether here or in realms beyond mortal knowledge. It does not seem to me unworthy to hope that the devil himself may be saved. But here indeed we work in inspired hope which may be fructified in faith by our own more perfect living. The final redemption of the created world from the bondage of sin, when the universe (to quote Romans 8.21) itself is to be freed from the shackles of mortality and enter upon the liberty and splendour of the children of God, is a mystery. But even as we act as mature, responsible human beings in the present moment, so we act to set in motion that great cosmic event. For the person of courage the present discontent also has its place in the divine scheme, and his way of ascent of the dark mountain is also a way to the divine knowledge; the pearl is revealed in the darkness no less than brilliantly concealed in the grandeur of life's pageant. Nothing is outside the range of God's healing love once it is brought to him in child-like trust. This is the basis of a living faith. No one can claim the hidden treasure until he has experienced and mastered the baser elements of life.

Again we are told to use our worldly wealth to win friends for ourselves, so that when money is a thing of the past we may be received into an eternal home (Luke 16.9). This statement, part of the Parable of the Dishonest Steward, is preceded by the observation that the worldly are more astute than the other-worldly in dealing with their own kind. The truly wise of the world — far removed from the merely worldly-wise, who are experts in managing affairs to their own temporal advantage but have little extended vision of the consequences of their actions in a broader framework of existence — can strike a balance between the current affairs of the world and the life of eternity. This we are living now also, however unaware we may be in our short-sighted actions of the passing scene. The two worlds, the visible and the invisible, are brought together in the realm of values: what is true, noble, just and pure, lovable and gracious, excellent and admirable (to quote Philippians 4.8), lifts our present situation into the world of eternity where there is no change, and where all creatures live together in a state of peace that passes all understanding.

In this state the cloud and the fire become one also, for now the light can be seen directly without any ensuing blindness. Conversely, the cloud is seen to contain the light of God as it too draws us on. It spurs us to our inspired efforts of understanding: scientific, social, economic and political. As we work with integrity in the deep mines of the world, impure as they (and we) may be, we contribute our service to the raising of the world, and when we die there will be many to greet us on the other side of life.

5 The Hollow Image

In the Creation Story we learn that God created man in his own image; when the free choice given to man was used in blind irresponsibility, the image was cracked as the human lurched convulsively on to the hard, pitiless ground of earthly solidity. Through divine grace the form of the image has been put together again but behind the imposing outer facade there lies a gaping void. The inner man is hollow and liable to be possessed by any invading force. The vision of the pearl brings him once more to himself and points to the way of full healing. Healing in this context can be envisaged as a re-creation of the human being in the divine image so that he can start to share in the very being of God.

The further we proceed, the more abruptly are we arrested in our tracks by sharp stabs of inadequacy as our dark shadow side comes to the fore in various guises. The greater our journey, the more familiar appears the landscape, drab, unrelieved by light and full of past failings that show no clear amelioration the more closely they are examined in the pitiless scrutiny of honest sight. There is a calculating insincerity about so much of our apparent progress. The path to the pearl traverses the unwholesome terrain of our own sickness. From time to time we may be so overcome with the hopelessness of the enterprise as to doubt whether we have in fact made any movement at all. And then we see, as if by direct divine intervention, that it is not our business to assess spiritual progress or to measure the extent, if any, of our inner cleansing. The ego consciousness that looks for results, paradoxically by its very insistence, blocks them at every turn; and yet, the doubt is the advance. The disillusion is also the ground of the humility that provides the energizing force moving us onwards in the great work ahead of us. The path is littered with artificial gem-stones, paste masquerading as pearls in their own right. Their presence challenges our own powers of discrimination, for what to one person may be the very light of God can be seen as the false glitter of illusion to a more acute observer. Amongst these false lights are gnostic teachings that promise a quick way to the final destination, demanding of us in turn an unquestioning obedience to the source that brings with it a complete surrender of the critical faculty of the mind. Also included are psychic intimations selfishly sought that, even if they are at times confirmed by later events, somehow interfere with our spontaneous responses to immediate events. Well does Jesus remind us all tha. each day has troubles enough of its own and that we should not be anxious about tomorrow, rather letting it look after itself. It is our needle-pointed attention to the moment in hand that directs us on our way to the pearl. Self-seeking motives, no matter how well couched they may be in a religious or philanthropic framework, can also dazzle us with their inflated grandeur; what appears to be a genuinely disinterested act of charity is soon exposed in its naked egoism. The way to God divests us of all comfortable illusions as it reveals to us our true nature as clearly as it is known to him. The forthright, unsentimental dismantling of our comforting escape routes that protect us from self-knowledge — our shadow piety and calculated conformity — leave us shivering and humiliated in the crisp, cold night air. Then, when the pain can scarcely be tolerated any longer, the pearl of great price declares itself, shedding its directive light upon us, like the sun suddenly emerging from behind a thick mass of clouds, and impels us onwards to proceed with the great work, leaving all behind us that offers spurious comfort at the cost of inner development. All that remains is the faith to live in child-like trust and open wonder at the glory of the present moment. When we find ourselves scarcely tolerable, we are amazed to be embraced in the everlasting arms of God, not only consoled as little children, but also given the strength to continue the work of claiming possession of the pearl, so tantalizingly within our grasp and yet so deceptively remote from us.

An especially dangerous snare on the path is our subservience to the canons of the world's approval and our dependence on the rewards this servitude promises. Indeed, our faulty evaluation of worldly rewards can lead to our equating them with the destination, the end of our seeking. The reward can, in other words, easily be mistaken for the pearl that lies at the heart of divine knowledge. It is in this respect particularly that we cannot serve God and the things of this world at the same time, inasmuch as the earthly recompense will be equated with the divine presence, thereby becoming a vain idol. We cannot advance at the same time as looking back to see what effect our efforts are having on others, and what rewards they are preparing for us. As Jesus puts it, no one who sets his hand to the plough and then keeps looking back is fit for the kingdom of God (Luke 9.62). It is the past associations of our lives that tempt us to look back and in them we seek the appropriate scale of rewards we hope to receive in the future. The possibility that the reward lies in the present moment itself with all that is achieved in that moment eludes us, as in our state of emotional stress and blind unawareness we are diverted into seeking material recompense. It is our divided consciousness that misleads us into paying too much attention to worldly views about success to the occlusion of our deeper spiritual vision. This becomes so befogged by the things of the world that emotional reactions cloud the cool judgement of clear reason. Spiritual aspiration is swept summarily into the corner, where it is left to smoulder like a burnt-out log. It follows therefore that an essential lesson on the way is the control of emotional upsurges. They have to be confronted, accepted for what they are, and then quietly laid aside. We have, in other words, to detach ourselves from emotional interference. As its dangerously destructive potential is neutralized, so we attain an inner release that allows us to do the work ahead of us with calm enjoyment. We return to something of the innocent child that we were many years previously, the child indeed we have to become before we can enter the kingdom of heaven where the pearl shines in undimmed radiance, awaiting our arrival and acceptance. At this juncture we no longer need to compare either ourselves or our particular contribution with anyone or anything outside ourselves; then we can keep our tensed arms steady to bear the emotional stress of everyday living as we proceed directly towards the divine presence. Thus we learn that it is our emotional turmoil that obscures our vision, especially the vision of God, remote and yet closer to us than our own soul, our intimate identity. For it is in God that we realize our identity as the spirit within us lights up the soul that encloses it.

Two episodes in the gospel are especially relevant to this theme: the path is also the destination and those whose attention wanders away from the path drift off into unprofitable realms of discontent. The first is the Parable of the Labourers in the Vineyard (Matthew 20.1-16): in this unusual story some of the workers are taken on at crack of dawn at an agreed wage, while others are hired at later times of the day up to an hour before the close of work. The employer then proceeds to pay all the labourers, starting with the late-comers and then moving on to those who had done a full twelve hours' stretch. To their indignation they discover that their fellows, who had done only one hour's work, received exactly the same payment as they who had toiled the whole working-day. Indeed, it seems grossly unfair as they grumble to the employer, but he dismisses them without ado, observing that he has fulfilled his side of the contract with them; how much he decides to pay the others is his business alone.

We cannot fail to sympathize with the early labourers: they seem somehow to have deserved something more in comparison with the later arrivals. Is there any way in which their disappointment could have been softened? As in all great stories we are surveying a multifaceted diamond of wisdom; so many different lessons can be learned from a quiet meditation on it. But one aspect is obvious: the early toilers were quite happy with the arrangement until they were joined by those coming later in the day. It was only when they compared their remuneration with that of those others that their content was shattered and they became angry with disappointment. If only they had kept their minds on their own affairs and not involved themselves with matters outside their concern!

But it may be argued, if this is the way of things, there seems no special advantage in honest, industrious labour; the ones who do a trifle get as much as those who work long and diligently. In fact the early workers have a distinct advantage over those who join them later in the day. The advantage is the dignity of honest labour and the sense of identity, of self-affirmation, that employment confers on those who are about some business. Compared with them, those who drifted around aimlessly until being offered work later were at a disadvantage, a state of affairs especially pertinent to our contemporary situation with its desolation of mass unemployment. Self-respect is closely related to a person's contribution to the society in which he lives; his employment is a source of justifiable self-esteem. To have no apparent place in the functioning of one's society is an implicit rejection no matter how generously one is cared for by the state. Self-esteem cannot be induced by gifts from outside; it depends on the actualization of one's personality so that one feels one's contribution is important in the general flow of events around one. Employment, in other words, has two functions; remuneration and dignity of office. The former is most immediately pertinent, but the latter is ultimately even more significant because it confirms a person's status in the community and the value of his life to those around him in the wider world.

The parable has in fact a wider application. Though the people of Israel are the children of the old covenant, and it is through them that Christ is incarnated, they have no special claims of advantage over the gentiles when the new covenant is promulgated. Their privilege was to be God's chosen people for a special event in the history of humanity's salvation. Nothing could be added by way of reward to that privilege. The same lesson has to be learnt by Jeremiah, chosen by God at an early age as his special prophet, but subject to unremitting hatred and persecution by the very people he had been sent to save from their persistent folly. God did not relieve his sufferings to any noticeable extent: he was simply told to get on with the work and stop grumbling even when his life was in mortal danger. If he persisted in self-commiseration, God would simply dispense with his services and select another prophet in his place. In fact, God's chosen ones cannot escape their vocation any more than could the rebellious Jonah by travelling to the ends of the earth to flee from his duty. But if they persist in faith, even when reviled by all their fellows, a new consciousness will dawn upon them so that the eternity of love will break open their self-imposed shell of rebellious grievance. And so the peak of Jeremiah's work is the prophecy of the new covenant to be written on the hearts of God's people, so that they will know him intuitively without the need of teaching from without (Jeremiah 31.31-4). To have been the mouthpiece of such a prophecy was infinitely more important in terms of the future of mankind than all the plaudits of his contemporaries, in much the same way as the truly enduring reward of a great artist is the appreciation that future generations will bestow on his name in loving gratitude. In such a situation even the promises of heaven in the life beyond death can be seen in their proper perspective as continued work on God's behalf for the whole aspiring, created universe. Virtue is its own reward; when it looks for its due recompense among the events of mundane life, it ceases to be virtue and shows itself instead as calculated manipulation of moral values for the sake of personal advancement. The end is either dishonesty or disappointment.

The second illustration of this principle is the simple story of Jesus with Martha and her sister Mary (Luke 10.38-42). While Martha was distracted by her many tasks, Mary sat imperturbably at the Lord's feet listening in rapt attention to his words. The more immediate task confronting Martha was preparing the meal for her guest, and we can with reason assume that this is what she was doing on this occasion. Her manifest love for Jesus, shared by her sister, would have precluded her doing any other work during his stay with them in the house. It would indeed have contravened common courtesy to have absented herself from her guest in order to perform some routine domestic duty that separated her from him for any length of time. So while Mary was contemplating Jesus, Martha was about the business of preparing a meal for all three of them, a task well within her compass since the repast was likely to have been a simple one. One can sense Martha's increasing chagrin as she sees herself encumbered with the work in the kitchen, while her sister not only does nothing to help her, but is actually enjoying Jesus' company alone in undisturbed delight. One can almost feel Martha's indignation rising up within her as she prepares the meal and lays the table with unnecessary clatter in order to make her presence felt, even if at a distance. At last her exasperation explodes as she asks Jesus if he is unconcerned that she is left to do all the work on her own, and she tells him to send Mary out to lend a hand. I believe Jesus' famous response, 'Martha, Martha, you are fretting and fussing about so many things; but one thing is necessary. The part that Mary has chosen is best; and it shall not be taken away from her', is often misconstrued. It is often claimed Jesus is exalting contemplation above action, but such a distinction is superficial as well as of very dubious validity; Martha, who prepares the meal, is surely of as great importance as Mary who simply attends to Jesus with her tranquil presence. I am sure Jesus enjoyed a well-prepared meal in the course of his unceasing ministry of teaching and healing.

It was Martha's attitude that he was gently rebuking, not her work about the house which was no doubt of exemplary quality. She was seeking acknowledgement and appreciation for all she was doing, yet all her labour seemed to be taken for granted and its strain ignored. If only she had kept her attention completely fixed on the domestic work with, as a concession, a pleasant thought about the final product of the meal together, she would have been completely happy, but instead she projected her imagination to the room where Mary and Jesus were alone together, and then brooded over all the bliss that she could not share with them. But the real bliss consisted in preparing the meal for their beloved master. In that frame of mind she would have been as close to Mary and Jesus as if she were sitting quietly in the room with them. She did not realize the privilege that she was given in being able to prepare a meal at all in the first case, and one especially for Jesus in the second. In comparing our lot with that of others we sacrifice the joy of our own existence in the present moment. God is everywhere, even if certain places and occasions focus his presence especially on our attention.

As regards the question of contemplation versus action, I believe there is at the heart of the matter a false antinomy. In fact, contemplation is the highest form of action, because the mind is directed, in the silence of the present moment, to the divine presence. Prayer is defined by the scholastics as the ascent of the mind to God. This ascent moves beyond conceptual images to the darkly dazzling silence where we wait in confident trust for our Lord to reveal himself. This he does with unfailing regularity even if we are so surrounded by the darkness of depression that, like Jesus on the cross, we feel he has forsaken us. But the supreme action of contemplative prayer proceeds according to our will and dedication to the great task, the claiming of the pearl which also embraces the vision of God. Sometimes we feel a heavenly sense of exaltation, sometimes nothing at all. Faith and love keep us about the work as we begin to learn that feelings and psychic impressions, intriguing though they may be, can as easily get in the way of our spiritual advance as illuminate the path ahead of us.

What we learn in the action of contemplation it is our duty and privilege to carry out in our worldly vocation. Then, like Brother Lawrence, we may say 'The time of business does not with me differ from the time of prayer; and in the noise and clutter of the kitchen, while several persons are at the same time calling for different things, I possess God in as great tranquillity as if I were upon my knees at the Blessed Sacrament', a declaration of spiritual contemplation in action that ends the Fourth Conversation of the little book *The Practice of the Presence of God*. In this respect it may be remembered that the person in question was called Nicholas Herman, a Frenchman of lowly birth who, after his service as a solidier and a footman, was admitted a lay brother in a community of Carmelites in Paris in 1666 where he was afterwards known as Brother Lawrence. A humble person of limited intellectual attainment, he was sent to serve in the convent's kitchen, a kind of work not especially congenial to him, but he persisted in his way of spiritual practice, marked especially by his endeavours to do everything as in the presence of God.

St Teresa of Avila, who too could find God easily among the pots and pans of her kitchen, wrote that 'to give our Lord a perfect hospitality, Mary and Martha must combine'. I would myself concentrate that observation: the two sisters have to become, in essence, a single person. Then we can see how perfect action is possible only as a consequence of perfect contemplation, while perfect contemplation fulfils itself in the angry world by perfect action. Only when the ego, with its innate craving for recognition, praise, recompense and security, is subdued can the person begin to act with a truly disinterested service that is the full measure of love. Then alone does truth guide the action, which no longer strives for the approval of others, but gets on with the work to God's greater glory and the benefit of the neighbour, who is everyone encountered in everyday life.

The hollow image is characterized by its clinging to diversions of earthly comfort, praise, reputation and reward. When it is shriven of these delights, its terrifying emptiness can at last be filled with the love of God in whose will alone is our peace, as Dante wrote in the Paradise section of *The Divine Comedy*. That will, however, does not overwhelm us either as an oracle or the voice of an imperious despot. It is the courteous still small voice that spoke to Elijah on Mount Horeb (or Sinai), where previously Moses too had received the divine commission to bring the law of righteousness to the people. When we are, like the exhausted Elijah, empty of self, we are ready to receive the divine power, which is in fact the real reward for true service whether to God or simply to our fellow creatures. In respect of service the two are essentially one, in much the same way that the first great commandment, to love God, is inseparably linked to the second, to love our neighbour as ourself.

6   The Way of Awareness

The problem of so much human endeavour, so much inadequacy that eats into years of life and renders them void of content, is the lack of awareness of the one who is called. Each day we are called by God to do our work to the fullness of our capacity, to live the present moment in its divine glory, to grow into wisdom and love through a direct participation of the circumstances that mark out the present scene, and to act as agents of renewal of all that is unclean around us. But we see nothing of this greater plan of creation amid the distraction of our present situation. We fail to appreciate the constant unfolding of opportunity that is the very nature of life because we are wrapped up in our own limited, unproductive fantasy world. This world is often peopled with creatures of darkness, the progeny of smouldering resentment and menacing fear. At other times we conjure up scenes of delight in order to flee from our own distress. If only we could see clearly like the man born blind, in John 9, who could say after his healing by Jesus, 'All I know is this: once I was blind, now I can see'! Those who interrogated him, men of strong religious faith but beset by emotional blockages and dogmatic preconceptions, could see nothing except the bare physical features of a changed man. We see the pearl as our intimation of a world of enduring values, but how rapidly does the mundane view occlude that vision, how rapidly do we return to past, unproductive ways of thinking! The coarse flesh hems in the spiritual emanations of the soul until such time as the carnal nature is humbled and shown its rightful place in the scheme of regeneration, that it must be still and listen instead of looking for its own satisfaction. It is the weakness of the flesh that is both our impediment and our way of spiritual growth. To hold fast to the pearl and the diversions of the world — the gnawing lust of the flesh and the temptations of the evil one, who is working towards a complete disintegration of the personality as a step towards the annihilation of the universe —

is the test of our integrity, the measure of our persistence in the face of daily discouragement.

In the first of the twin verses of the *Dhammapada*, the Buddha writes:

> All that we are is the result of what we have thought: it is founded on our thoughts and made up of our thoughts. If a man speak or act with an evil thought, suffering follows him as the wheel follows the hoof of the beast that draws the wagon . . . If a man speak or act with a good thought, happiness follows him like a shadow that never leaves him.

But in order to attain this state of blessed equanimity which is the prerequisite for the spiritual life, there must be the practice of silence before the Creator. When we are still, even if encompassed by chaos and threatened by the hostility of those close to us, the power of the Holy Spirit infuses us and shows us the reality that underlies all phenomenal appearances. In this state of 'holy indifference' we can initiate a series of right actions, for it is no longer merely we who are responding, but the power of the Creator working through us. He lightens our path by his spiritual radiance, and then the pearl is seen as a diadem on the heavenly throne. In other words, the act of thought that both the Buddha and St Paul (in Philippians 4.8, as we have already noted) emphasize as the true basis of the spiritual life, finds its consummation in deep contemplative silence before God, however we may know the divine principle of eternal creation. Thus we read the Buddha's teaching about the first and ultimate cause of all, 'There is an unborn, not become, not made, uncompounded, and were it not for this unborn, not become, not made, uncompounded, no escape could be shown here from what is born, has become, is made, is compounded.'

To be aware of God at all times ensures our conscious participation in the phenomenal universe with all that impinges directly upon us. To be unresponsive to the divine dispensation that protects us day by day, lays us open to the invasion of our consciousness by subversive forces in the intermediate, psychic realm that interpenetrates the present moment. If we give of our best, we will receive the highest reward, the essence of which is the power to continue with the great work. The Christian would extend the Buddha's teaching about the ground of all existence by finding love as its central core. In this way the measureless, incomprehensible void, that is the Godhead, shows itself in the world of becoming — in which we are all to grow into the fullness of our own being, the height of the stature of our individual integrity — as love. This love cares for all its creatures equally, both in their present individual mode and in their collective dispersion as the body of the universe. Meister Eckhart said, 'Why do you prate of God? Whatever you say is wrong.' The great mystics of the world know that the deity is neither this nor that, while at the same time being both this and that, the coincidence of opposites that Nicholas of Cusa glimpsed. In needle-pointed awareness the totality of existence is both apprehended and transcended as the divine light shines upon the intellect, so that it is transformed into an instrument of active receptivity. It can assimilate the divine light and transmit its essence to the world in rational categories. This is the great moment of decision ahead of the seeker of the pearl of great price, a renunciation of the way of known transit for a passage that is hidden from the sight of mortal travellers on the path. Yet how often do we lose the strand of immediate awareness and its consequences even in the course of a single day! Two episodes from the gospel stand out particularly in this respect. In one, quoted in Luke 17.11-19, as Jesus was entering a village he was met with ten men who had a disfiguring skin disease, termed leprosy in the common translation, but probably a condition different from the well-known disease of that name. But one thing was certain: the sufferer was taboo from the remainder of the community. He had to identify himself publicly, was ritually unclean, and had to live apart and stay outside the settlement (Leviticus 13.45-6). Cruel as this seems, it was also a primitive health precaution and should be judged accordingly, as should much of the Mosaic code that appears so strange to modern minds. The ten victims called on Jesus, from some way off, to have pity on them. At once they were healed of their disfigurement. But only one, an outcast Samaritan, had the gratitude to come back to Jesus and give thanks to God for what he had received. The nine Jews, sons of the covenant, had so forgotten their past suffering in the face of their present cure that it never occurred to them to give thanks for what they had received; and they are typical of many sick people who take their medical cure for granted and never so much as think of giving thanks, not only to the doctors and medical ancillaries, but to God himself. They might, of course, retort that it was God who laid the burden of illness on them in the first place, and so it was his business — almost his duty — to see to their healing. Only a deeper awareness of their past attitudes and actions might begin to clear their inner vision so that their own responsibility in their illness became more apparent to them. And even if their own lives had been impeccably virtuous, they would still have to learn that no man lives to himself alone, for we are all members of a greater community. In the famous words of John Donne, 'No man is an island, entire of itself. Any man's death diminishes me, because I am involved in mankind. And therefore never send to know for whom the bell tolls; it tolls for thee.' So the suffering of even a distant neighbour has its repercussion on those afar off.

I suspect that the outcast, heretical Samaritan, the only one who flowed out to Jesus in thanksgiving, knew this truth, even if he could not have articulated it so roundly. When we too are left on the ground struggling for life, like the assaulted, robbed man in the Parable of the Good Samaritan, certain basic facts of life strike our aware mind, aware because it is singularly free from worldly distractions and can now concentrate on the one thing that matters, that is, the divine presence that never leaves us even when we leave it for more immediately attractive pursuits. The Samaritan leper knew that he was an unworthy individual in his own right — as indeed we all are — but was nevertheless taken up in love by God, revealed in Jesus, and miraculously healed. This is the basic Christian experience, and at once it converts us from a devotion to secular things to a dedication of ourselves to God, revealed definitively in the person of Jesus. What later generations of Christians were to know as an inner experience, was shown to this man, poor in reputation, yet rich in grace. He was made aware while the nine Jewish lepers remained as unconscious of God's love afterwards as they had been before.

The story is an appropriate complement to the Parable of the Good Samaritan, where once again it is the outcast who helps the stricken traveller, while the pillars of religious propriety walk in oblivious selfishness on the other side of the road, lest their inner deliberations be disturbed by their fellow man in need. It could well be that the healed Samaritan was destined later to be the good Samaritan who acted with charity in the famous parable. The episode also shows us the vast distance that separates the cure of a disease from the healing of the whole person; the nine were as far from that healing after Jesus' work as before it, while the solitary outcast was at least on the right road. Jesus' healings were a manifestation of the imminence of the kingdom of God, but not all who received the healing opened themselves up to the greater gift of God's undemanding love. The tragedy of love lies in the frequently negative response in those to whom it is given. Until they are inwardly aware, love simply flows through them like water in a sieve, or else they reject it out of hand. Free will is God's supreme gift to us but its use entails an enormous responsibility. It is for this reason that physical and mental healing are preferably gradual, so that the patient can learn to cope with their implications in slow stages. In the same way the person suddenly left a large legacy may find it a burden rather than a cause for rejoicing. He is, at any rate, more likely to spend it improvidently than invest it wisely for his own good and the benefit of the community. The person who has felt the full impact of poverty and family responsibility will have a much more sober attitude to gifts of money.

The other teaching in the gospel that reminds us how soon we forget a gift because of our lack of self-awareness, and of the consequences that this forgetfulness can have, is contained in the Parable of the Unforgiving Debtor (Matthew 18.23-35). In this story, a man who owes his master an enormous amount of money and has no means of repaying the debt, is threatened with being sold into slavery together with his entire family. But because of his terrible distress and his undertaking to pay everything back when he can, the master is so filled with compassion that he releases the debtor absolutely. But later on in the day this same man encounters a fellow-servant who owes him a trifle by comparison with his own debt. Despite the other man's pleas for time to redress the debt, the servant remains adamant in his grasping fury and has his debtor summarily imprisoned. The other servants, not surprisingly, are most distressed over the episode, and tell the whole tale to the master. He then confronts the first servant with his lack of gratitude which should have been reflected in mercy to his debtor, but instead had flared up into insatiable greed. And so the first servant was condemned to torture until he could pay the full amount of his debt, a very unlikely event in view of its magnitude. It is interesting that Jesus compares this sorry story to the kingdom of heaven; it has something therefore to tell us about the ultimate dispensation of things in the eternity of existence that far outdistances our relatively short span of life on earth. The first servant is a typical man of the world, squealing when he is hurt, but as ungrateful after his relief as if nothing at all had happened to him. As he was able to accept the gift of mercy and retain a sense of gratitude for merely a moment in time, so his experience of heaven was as limited in duration. And then an indefinite hell of pain awaited him. One hopes that somehow he was able to pay the debt in full — and here our perspective may widen from mere money to his whole life as dedicated in service to his fellow creatures — but the time taken for spiritual growth to occur would be very long. It gives us a graphic account of hell and an intermediate state of purgation of evil impulses from the chastened personality. It also reminds us how dangerous it can be to remove an impediment from a person until he is able to hold on to the release he has been given.

Jesus illustrates this vividly in his story of an evil spirit that leaves a person for a span to rest in the desert. When it returns to its victim, it finds the house unoccupied, swept clean and tidy, so off it goes to collect seven other spirits more wicked than itself. They all come in and settle down, so that in the end the person's plight is worse than before (Matthew 12.43-5). The power who should have occupied the cleansed psyche of the person was the Holy Spirit, but he does not enter automatically to fill the vacuum left by the departure of another occupant. He has to be invited to come in, since God's approach to us is always one of courtesy, as befits a creature to whom he has given a free will. The Holy Spirit enters us almost as a bodily presence when we call upon the name of the Lord in rapt prayer; then our awareness is acute and undefiled, so that we can with authority discern between the Spirit of God and various dubious inhabitants of the intermediate, psychic realm who would be pleased to personate God and enter into the sacred domain of the individual personality. In other words, until we are so filled with the love of God that his presence is with us as a conscious power at all times, we are liable to fall victim not only to impulses deeply set in our own unconscious but also to psychic debris around us that is only too available to infest us.

It is, in this respect, no surprise that a person not infrequently falls victim to one misfortune after another until his eyes are opened to the flaw in his own psyche that allows discord and disorder to erupt in his life. Even if we were, in the company of most contemporary psychologists and theologians, to dismiss the concept of entity-possession out of hand as a primitive superstition, we can still understand how one disaster after another can punctuate a vulnerable person's existence until he learns to take charge positively of his life. Practitioners of the power of positive thinking stress this truth with special vigour, but in the end it is God, rather than the individual, who is in charge. Therefore positive thinking, to be truly effective, should be grounded in prayer, the dialogue of the soul with God. Personally, I have little doubt about the possibility of invasion of the personality by external psychic forces both from the living and the dead. But I can see only too clearly how such a belief can so dominate a person's thinking that all untoward phenomena are attributed to external agencies in the intermediate dimension. In this way human responsibility is progressively eroded, while all those who challenge the individual's security and threaten the slender faith by which he lives can be identified with the powers of darkness and then mercilessly persecuted. A sense of balance founded on acute awareness is essential in assessing the cause of all human, and indeed cosmic, disorder. This balance is the product of prayer and responsible conduct in the present moment.

Awareness is closely linked with caution on the one hand and gratitude on the other. The caution is part of the body's defence against foolish, ill-judged actions that would endanger its integrity. The inborn fear of death that we all have, no matter how vigorously we may deny it on an intellectual level, is the body's insistence of its own right of survival. Without that built-in caution we would endanger our lives day by day in foolhardy ventures, and all too probably die prematurely. We, in this context, reflect on Jesus' words in respect of his healing of the man who was born blind, 'While daylight lasts we must carry on the work of him who sent me; night comes, when no one can work. While I am in the world I am the light of the world' (John 9.4-5). It would be no blasphemy if we all were to identify ourselves with Jesus in this saying, for we are all unique lights in our own setting, when we are functioning as complete people. It is for this reason that our time on earth is so important; convinced as I am that mortal existence is but a parenthesis in eternity, I also am sure that this time on earth is vitally important in executing work and experiencing relationships that cannot be provided in any other realm of existence. The physical body is both our vehicle of self-expression and our organ of limitation. Time limits the extent of our growth, and its interruption in death cuts off our deepest relationships and emphasizes the necessity for renunciation at every moment. Space limits the scope of our endeavours, and as the body fails, so we are confined to an ever-diminishing domain. Here we have to serve the world, ultimately in prayer alone, as our faculties gradually decline with the attrition wrought by ageing and disease. As St Paul was told in the trial wrought by his persistent 'thorn in the flesh' that resisted all prayers for healing, 'My grace is all you need; power comes to its full strength in weakness' (2 Corinthians 12.9).

In this respect we remember the dictum of the Wisdom teaching of the Old Testament: the fear of the Lord is wisdom, and to turn from evil is understanding (Job 28.28). This fear is not an attitude of terror at the unpredictable moods of a powerful despot, whose wrath may flare out against us at any moment if we, even unwittingly, offend him. It is rather a sense of awe that we have been privileged to be where we are, doing what we are to do, at this present moment, in an infinity of space and an eternity of time. 'When I look up at thy heavens, the work of thy fingers, the moon and the stars set in their places by thee, what is man that thou shouldst remember him, mortal man that thou shouldst care for him? Yet thou has made him little less than a god, crowning him with glory and honour' (Psalm 8.3-5), or again, 'Thou it was who didst fashion my inward parts; thou didst knit me together in my mother's womb. I will praise thee for thou dost fill me with awe; wonderful thou art, and wonderful thy works' (Psalm 139.13-14). In our lives the awe of God is closely linked with our gratitude in being alive as human beings. In this frame of mind we can begin to understand the statement in the Genesis story that God created man, male and female, in his own image. Our perspective rises from purely material considerations of daily sustenance to the infinite glory of life itself; we move beyond personal concern to universal benediction and flow out rapturously in love to all God's creatures. It is thus that there is a living synthesis of awe and gratitude; indeed the two responses seem almost to unite to form a new awareness of reality.

God is love, and wrath is not in his nature. The wrath of suffering is due to a contravention of basic laws of life by which God governs his universe. If we disobey those laws, we suffer accordingly. Just as promiscuous sexual habits bring in their train disastrous venereal disorders, and excesses of alcohol, drugs and tobacco, their quota of progressive damage to various organs of the body, so do deceitful actions and treacherous betrayals of trust of intimate relationships lead to strife and conflict. But if we have the honesty to confess our shortcomings and genuinely work towards a nobler style of life, the forgiveness of God helps us to attain a new relationship with the world and a peak of service to our fellows. In the words of Dame Julian of Norwich:

> For I saw no wrath but on man's part, and that forgiveth he us. For wrath is not else but a frowardness and contrariness to peace and love; and either it cometh of failing of might, or of failing of wisdom, or of failing of goodness: which failing is not in God, but is on our part (*Revelations of Divine Love*, Chapter 8).

The 'frowardness and contrariness' here described are best understood as a perverse antagonism to peace and love. This seems to be the cumulative effect of persistent disobedience to the divine law on the part of God's rational creatures and the suffering that accrues from this rebelliousness. It may need a complete shattering of the individual's fortunes to arrest this fatal trend, a situation well illustrated in the Parable of the Prodigal Son, when the young man comes to his true being only in the midst of penury. Then at last he enters full awareness both of his situation and the way to proceed from its consequences.

The battle between the self-will of the rational creature and the divine will that cares for all creatures without discrimination is also the way of growth of the individual. The end of this battle is not so much a triumph of God's love over personal selfishness as an acceptance, a taking-up of the personal into the transpersonal. There are no lasting victors in any conflict, since the fire of the storm continues to smoulder, albeit beneath the surface, until the conflagration erupts anew. In the end all parties have to be satisfied, and each is then embraced in the all-accepting love of God, in which love there is a transmutation of the base, selfish elements into instruments of world service. We are to come to God as self-aware, responsible people, not as trembling slaves at the feet of an awesome tyrant. Then we can give something valuable of ourselves to him, namely the unique character that we have forged and attained through our confrontation with pain in the vicissitudes of our individual lives.

> For all who are moved by the Spirit of God are sons of God. The Spirit you have received is not a spirit of slavery leading you back to a life of fear, but a spirit that makes us sons, enabling us to cry 'Abba, Father'. In that cry the Spirit of God joins with our spirit in testifying that we are God's children; and if children, then heirs (Romans 8:14-16).

We may remember in this respect that 'Abba, Father' was the way in which Jesus started his prayer for relief from his suffering at Gethsemane, which ended in an acceptance of his Father's will (Matthew 26.42). It is above all else a declaration of responsibility, of adult stature, one in which we can co-operate in loving sevice with God and our fellow creatures. The intimation of glory in the vision of the pearl is the presage of this maturity, but it has to be actualized in the less exalted situations of everyday life.

We have to accept that our life on earth is fraught with danger and suffering no less than relief and joy. Each experience is a stepping-stone towards completion of the person into something of the stature of Christ. We not unnaturally look for happiness and ease, but the adverse states have also to be

experienced so that our spiritual endurance may be strengthened. In this vein St Paul compares the spiritual way with that
of an athlete contending for an earthly prize, but, as he says, the
prize in store for the asceticism of the spiritual aspirant is out of
all comparison with earthly rewards. When we understand this,
we cease to rail against the injustice of our fate, and instead, like
the chastened Jeremiah, get on with the work with renewed
determination.

When Job was smitten with misfortune, his wife told him to
curse God and die. He in turn made the important observation,
'If we accept good from God, shall we not accept evil?' (Job
2.10). While it is intolerable that a God of love should deliberately visit pain on his creatures, there can be no doubt of the
immensity of the scale of evil in the world. This is most
satisfactorily attributed to the perverse attitudes and actions of
the rational forms of life and the power they wield. But these
same creatures have bequeathed to those who succeeded them
a treasury of music, art, literature, philanthropic endeavour and
scientific knowledge. We take all this as a matter of course
whenever we attend a concert or listen to the radio, visit an art
gallery or read a classic of world literature. Likewise the
enormous technical advances in medical science have added
years of life and mobility to those many who would have
succumbed early to the ravages of heart disease or been
painfully crippled with osteo-arthritis which so often afflicts
older people. The contributions of the few have added beyond
measure to the span and quality of the lives of great multitudes.
Likewise do we have to bear our share of the world's terrible
agony, so close is human solidarity, even when it is obvious that
we ourselves are innocent victims of violence as part of the blind
injustice and cruelty of the society in which we live. The
emotionally balanced person can bear the implications of the
inter-relatedness of all life, this coinherence of consciousness in
each member of the group. He can appreciate the privilege of
suffering in union with the wretched of the earth no less than
that of exulting in the glory of the world's great achievements.
St Paul writes, 'It is now my happiness to suffer for you. This is
my way of helping to complete, in my poor human flesh, the full
tale of Christ's afflictions still to be endured for the sake of his
body which is the church' (Colossians 1.24). What is thus

assumed in love is transferred in prayer to God: the suffering is
no longer retributive but is now redemptive of the whole
created universe, a suffering fully known in the passion of
Christ. We are, in other words, heirs of both the light and the
darkness of the world, and as we accept their totality, so we
grow in stature as people who can ease the way forward for the
world's transfiguration into a kingdom of light in whose midst
there radiates the precious pearl. Just as we contain an inbuilt
pattern of growth in our personality, so too does the world have
its own scheme of development. It too has its times of natural
disasters in the form of earthquakes, floods and droughts which
affect the lives of all who live in it. Every now and then a tower
of Siloam collapses on some hapless victims. They are killed
while the previously unaware bystanders are jolted out of their
blind complacency and made alert of the precarious nature of all
life and its precious quality (Luke 13.4-5). We take the order of
the cosmos for granted until some natural disaster opens our
eyes to our membership of and dependence on the whole
universe. Can we do anything to ameliorate severe natural
disasters, which, after all, are simply an indication that not only
we but the whole world are in a state of continuous creation?
Prayer for good weather conditions, especially during storms
and droughts, amuses the secular atheist by its childish
dependence on an illusory intelligence that is held to govern the
universe, but prayer nevertheless does seem to have an effect
remarkably quickly in some emergencies. It is not beyond
possibility that malaligned psychic currents emanating from
disturbed populations could have an adverse effect on the
earth's rhythms; concentrated prayer might then by its quiet
calmness reverse the disturbance and help to bring the elements
back into harmony. Of course, even if this hypothesis were to be
confirmed it would not deny the labile nature of the world and
its tendency to internal eruption as part of its price for growth. It
would simply stress the adverse effect that disturbed human
emotions and the psychic currents they produce may have on a
precariously balanced universal flux.

It seems that when we behave in awareness of the present
moment, much that is unpleasant is brought to light both in
ourselves and in the greater world. The unveiling of the face of
evil is the work of the Holy Spirit. We cannot turn back, but we

are assured of divine assistance in our journey onwards towards the great destination. As we walk in the awareness of God's presence, so we are strengthened to continue with work of lightening the darkness that is always around us. This is the work of the saints of all ages.

7 Diversions

The path to the summit of the mountain of transfiguration at whose apex lies the pearl of great price is lined by side-tracks with wide, welcoming entrances that promise intriguing destinations. We remember Jesus' admonition:

> Enter by the narrow gate. The gate is wide that leads to perdition, there is plenty of room on the road and many go that way; but the gate that leads to life is small and the road is narrow, and those who find it are few (Matthew 7.13-14).

If Jesus were alive in the flesh today, there would be many who would criticize him as an élitist, but we have nevertheless to come to terms with the evident truth that the wide gate that forms the entrance to the spacious road of self-indulgence and immediate satisfaction is crowded with life's travellers, whereas the narrow, rugged path up the towering mountain of spiritual proficiency is the preserve of the few, indeed the very few.

In this respect we can meditate once more on Jesus' famous Parable of the Sower and the Seed: some seed fell along the footpath and the birds devoured it. Some fell on rocky ground with little soil; it sprouted quickly enough because it had no depth of earth, but it soon withered under the scorching rays of the sun, as it had little root. Some fell among thistles, which shot up and choked the corn. But some fell into good soil, where it thrived and bore plentiful fruit (Matthew 13.4-8). It is interesting that Jesus spoke to the crowds in the esoteric language of the parable; only the disciples were privileged to hear the exoteric doctrine that animated the esoteric teaching, for none was capable of grasping the inner meaning of the parable directly. Jesus explains that the parable illustrated the way of entering the kingdom of God: some hear the word of God, symbolized by the seed which is always fertile, but fail to understand it, so that it is soon annulled by the seductive power of evil. Others hear and accept the word with joy, but do not respond by a radical change in lifestyle; they therefore have no power of endurance and cannot stand up to the travail and persecution that the word, by its truth, induces in the world around them, and so they soon drop away into the anonymous mass of humanity who mill around in mindless tumult. Others hear the word, but are soon diverted by the affairs of the world and its meretricious values; the word of life is choked in them and proves barren. But some are able to hear and understand the word so that it flourishes in the depth of their souls, where it brings forth a harvest of good works which set in action the transformation of society and the transfiguration of the world. This final category is a symbol of the Church with its staying-power in the face of dark discouragement and vicious persecution. In its moment of illumination it ceases to be a mere institution set to perpetuate itself, and starts to fulfil its vocation of service to all creation, invariably to its cost. The Church of God does not reject the world or its values; it rather works with it in order to enlighten it and heal the terrible sickness of humanity. Then the seed will flourish unfailingly and with profusion in the soil of common life.

If we could only see the details of the heavenly banquet, we would not be detained by earthly attractions. And there are many who have seen through the imposing facade of worldly triumphs to the terrible void that lies within them. They too seek the kingdom and its treasured pearl, but morbid impatience dominates their enthusiasm, and so they look for rapid individualistic ways to the common summit of the mountain of transfiguration. It must be said in their favour that they have seen the inadequacy of worldly riches in the great quest. They therefore do not hanker after money, prestige or the flattery that inflates the personality to a balloon-like stature. Instead they set their hearts on the acquisition of knowledge, the gnosis that can tap on the very gate of heaven and demand, even force, entrance. Surely, it might be argued, this is much to be commended: they have consecrated their very being to the great quest and they deserve the fruits of their labour. But what are those fruits, and how has their labour been expended? Are they trying to snatch the pearl from its heavenly seat, or are they sacrificing their very selves for the sake of its purchase? The difference between the two approaches to truth is vast, and yet to many unthinking seekers the ways almost coincide. There is, in fact, a gnosis of occult derivation that seeks to control the universe, and a divine gnosis that rests in the love of God. We remember once more the teaching in *The Cloud of Unknowing* that God can be attained in vision only by love, but not by thought alone. This statement is not to be seen as a disparagement of the rational faculty, for without it we would soon fall into every type of superstition and fanaticism. It is rather an assertion of the primacy of love and of the warmth of the soul, by which alone the rational faculty, the native intelligence, can be cleansed of emotional blockages and arid pride, and become the chastened vehicle whereby the intuitive knowledge is made available in the common life both of the individual and of the greater community. But we cannot know love until we have moved beyond the ego consciousness that demands recompense for its labours and rewards for its service. Thus we come to the circular argument: to know God you have to be empty of self, and yet this self-emptying can be effected only by the divine grace. How great a paradox is contained in this prescription of the spiritual life! It seems to depend on the movement of the soul, re-membering St Augustine's observation at the beginning of his *Confessions* that God has made us for himself alone and our souls are restless until they rest in him. There is something of God in all of us, and it is this principle that alone can lead us on to the divine encounter, when at last we can acquire the pearl as our own. But if the ego leads us, we shall soon find ourselves in a capacious cul-de-sac with many fellow travellers in a similar state of disillusion and fear. It may be like the Faust story of selling our souls to the devil.

We read in the Bible, 'If you invoke me and pray to me, I will listen to you: when you seek me you shall find me; if you search with all your heart, I will let you find me, says the Lord' (Jeremiah 29.12-13). Jesus amplifies this promise, 'Ask, and you will receive; seek, and you will find; knock, and the door will be opened. For everyone who asks receives, he who seeks finds, and to him who knocks, the door will be opened' (Matthew 7.7-8). Yet we know so well from our own experience how often we remain outside the kingdom and despite all our insistent knockings at the door of heaven. All our search seems vain, and not a few who have offered themselves to the sacred ministry have subsequently left, disillusioned and angry with the God who seems to take a special delight in hiding himself, as he appeared to do even to Jesus nailed pitifully to the cross of human malice. The secret of Jeremiah's prophecy seems to be 'searching with all the heart'. In other words the whole person — body, mind, soul and spirit — has to be consecrated to the search, in the course of which a total renunciation may be demanded. But this demand is from God and never from the individual, no matter how 'advanced' he may appear to be in spiritual knowledge, which is in fact more likely to be occult lore. Here we come to the crux of the matter. God looks for our assumption of the full image in which he created us, whereas human teachers of the occult gnostic mode and those who seek after it, yearn, albeit frequently unconsciously, for personal power. In fact both teacher and pupil are trapped in a cul-de-sac on the way. There they will remain indefinitely until they admit their error and seek the guidance that comes with absolution and forgiveness. God seeks the heart which he turns from stone to flesh.

If we seek from the vantage point of the ego, the very object of our search seems to elude our contact. The further we stretch out to acquire, the more insistently does the prize recede from our grasp. The same principle can be seen in human relationships. If an individual is cornered by an inquisitive interrogator and pressed to reveal his life story, that person is very likely to shut up like a clam. Something private and sacred is being exposed to the unrestricted gaze of the multitude. Not only is this intimate secret of the inner life coarsened and cheapened by verbalization, but the person himself is also denuded of something peculiar to himself and sacred in the inner eye of the soul; the further the interrogation proceeds, the less co-operative does the individual become, until eventually he reaches a point of obduracy due to both increasing embarrassment and mounting resentment. The inner mystery of a person is sacred, like the ground on which Moses stood as he experienced the presence of God within the burning bush. He was told to remove his shoes because the ground was especially holy, being infused by the divine presence. The bare feet of the prophet were to be in direct contact with God. In the same way we too have to be emptied of guile and every trace of self-seeking ambition before we can experience God's presence and the love that flows out from him. We indeed cannot serve two masters, God and the things of this world. Only when our attention to God is sharp and urgent can the divine power pour down upon us.

The attraction of secret knowledge is certainly powerful. Not only is the seeker promised an understanding of the hidden forces that govern outer events, but he is also enticed by the power such knowledge promises. It is especially the person low in self-esteem that finds the occult gnostic path attractive, for here at last he can feel important and find a security that eludes him in the course of his daily work. The ego always appreciates inflation, whether from fulsome flattery or the assurance of controlling powers beyond rational cognizance. Well did Jesus warn his disciples of the seductive power of flattery, for it was lavished on the false prophets of earlier times. The true prophet seldom evokes much gratitude because his message is full of truth, the truth that demolishes all private illusions of grandeur and communal illusions of special privilege. All these are subtle diversions that deflect the seeker away from the main path so as to bask in the admiration of the obtuse multitudes who cannot discriminate between gold and dross. They seek continually after a sign.

Is the way of the occultist, the quest after the roots of the psychic power that energizes the world, of any validity in the spiritual path, or is it purely a devil-sent diversion that separates the seeker from the final goal? Two questions need to be answered in this respect: do such occult powers and phenomena in fact exist, and if so, are their manifestation and control an indication of the spiritual proficiency of the seeker on the path? Do they, in essence, assist the search, or are they basically an obstruction in the way of spiritual progress? We may with advantage hearken back to the story of the Fall, when Adam and Eve submit to the temptation of eating the fruit of the tree of the knowledge of good and evil without prior reference of the matter to God, who had already instructed them to avoid eating the forbidden fruit. And yet he places the forbidden tree together with the beneficial tree of life in the middle of the garden of Eden. It can hardly seem possible that God wishes man to be eternally ignorant of the principles of moral judgement that form the basis of discriminating good from evil, but patience and discipline are called for until the time is ripe for the great leap forward under the aegis of God himself. Instead of waiting in obedient trust, the impulsive human plunges ahead under his own steam, and does indeed acquire the knowledge that gives him power over his immediate surroundings. But he has excluded God from his undertaking, and so everything he does subsequently is tainted with egoistic pride and selfish domination. The fruit of the tree of life is now excluded from his grasp, for his own cupidity has put him at enmity with the whole created order; the dominion granted him by virtue of his superior intellect has now become divisive and aggressive. The type of knowledge associated with the rational understanding, if it is not fertilized with love, soon becomes tyrannical and destructive. Without the love that is the very root of our relationship with God, all our intellectual aspirations founder on the rocks of discord and destruction. On the deeper level it seems to me that the fruit promised Eve by the devil was an initiation into the psychical dimension of power by which the world is animated. It embraces the hidden resources of God that are the basis of the great law of creation by which all order is established and all life maintained. That a sphere of knowledge exists that transcends purely rational categories is evident to many people in the course of their lives. Sudden flashes of information, apparently irrelevant and never consciously invoked, may come spontaneously either in the course of waking life with its dull routine of work to be performed or else during the dream life of sleep. This information is subsequently proved by the course of events to have been far from irrelevant, indicating that the unconscious has access to information relevant to times and places remote from the person's knowledge, often of frightening intensity. It is of interest that scientific investigations into the paranormal realm have been, at least to date, disappointingly equivocal. The phenomena are unpredictable and cannot be called upon to order. Their appearance resembles that of the Holy Spirit, who as Jesus tells Nicodemus, in their secret nocturnal meeting, blows where he wishes, just like the wind, whose sound can indeed be heard but whose origin and destination remain unpredictable (John 3.8). So it is with those who are filled with the Holy Spirit. There are societies that claim to be able to develop the normal, usually dormant, human psychic faculties, and there are also more ambitious groups that seek to unravel the secrets of the fabric of the universe, the scheme of individual life, death and rebirth in a supramundane context.

The property that these people share is a claim to a special power or knowledge outside the normal range — paranormal in fact — which can be attained by special disciplines. These mark the aspirant as someone outside the common run of mankind, and set him in action for mastery of a very special type. He not only knows the inner, hidden (or occult) meaning of the world's great scriptures, but also belongs to an élite, a coterie that has special powers, notably in the here and now but also in the greater life beyond death. It becomes increasingly obvious to the intelligent observer that the source of this 'secret doctrine', this theosophical dogma, is a psychical focus in the intermediate dimension, closely related to the souls of the departed and the angelic host. Both of these realms have their dark, grey and light areas. A little of what is imparted is of high spiritual calibre, much rather banal and tautological, and some of very dubious validity indeed. The living instrument, or channel, may be a medium in trance or a fully conscious communicator in control of the material. The phenomenon is especially seductive as it purports to come from the regions beyond death, as indeed appears on some occasions to be the case. But even if this origin is accepted, at least occasionally, does it confer on the teaching an especially illuminating authority? That mysterious teaching may come from a bona-fide source in the life beyond death does not guarantee its spiritual authenticity any more than its moral authority. If the soul does, as I believe, grow in understanding in the afterlife, it might take a long time (as far as we can conceive of time in the afterlife) for it to be the transmitter of any noteworthy spiritual teaching of a type not previously available in our more limited earthly plane. Jesus' criterion is one of fruits of actions and teachings, and the fruits of this realm are seldom of great spiritual value, such as we could not find better expressed in the world's treasury of scriptural writing with its product of saintly commentary in words and action. Where, in unusual instances, impressive dogma is transmitted, it leads the hearers back to fundamental spiritual sources already freely available to them, provided they have the interest and humility

to follow the leading of the Holy Spirit. The danger of all this is
that the aspirant is insidiously led into an enticing cul-de-sac
where the voice of the teacher assumes a god-like authority,
however much it may disclaim such a role. False modesty can be
much more persuasively captivating than demagogic rhetoric.
The more freedom offered in these regions, the more subtly is
the free will yielded for the sake of unquestioning obedience to
the occult teacher. The same criteria of unease apply to the
prophets of various pseudo-spiritual sects and cults. It is they
and what they proclaim that become the focus of authority. A
very dangerous idolatry takes control as the face of the pearl is
occluded by the cloud of gnostic speculation and psychical
confusion. The clear face of eternity known to the simple
contemplative, like, for instance, Brother Lawrence, is the proof
of the reliability of the way of prayer. The confused medley of
conflicting voices is the fruit of those who become enmeshed in
gnostic claims and arcane teachings that emanate from psychic
sources.

Can we therefore say that psychic intrusions are all evil? Is all
theosophical doctrine a dangerous diversion from the straight
path that leads to the vision of God, to the pearl of great price
that is our earnest of the divine providence? The answer, as in
all problems of this type, is neither a simple affirmative nor a
categorical negative. These dimensions of personality exist, and
in themselves are a means of relating the individual to sources of
creativity and feeling that lie beyond the personal field to unite
the whole creation in a bond of intimate relationship. The
highest bond is love, and if the psychic information has this
effect it is indeed a vehicle of grace. Usually, however, it
remains an ideal in its own right, so that it usurps the place of
the Deity in the life of the aspirant. People dedicated to the
pursuit of arcane knowledge find themselves cornered in a
blind alley until they renounce gnosis for its own sake and turn
to an orthodox religious tradition. Despite its periods of
darkness throughout the centuries, the way of religious
orthodoxy — and here we may speak in terms of all the great
traditions — is illuminated by the lives of its numerous saints,
and they alone are the trustworthy guides along the spiritual
path that leads to the pearl of great price. The occult path comes
to a halt as the end of the cul-de-sac is reached, and then it is

seen to be a trap except for those who have the humility and courage to repair their weary way back to the main highway.

On the other hand it must be conceded that a number of atheistic humanists have been led on to that highway through psychical experiences and contact with members of gnostic sects. Others have likewise returned to the Christian fold after illuminating encounters in the Hindu or Buddhist traditions, both of which possess a depth of understanding of the life of contemplation that even today is very often lacking in much Christian religious practice. The gnostic dimension is at least conversant with a span of life that is greater than merely the earthly one. Even if its rather forbidding schemes of rebirth find little sympathy in many Christian circles, at least they encourage the adventurous seeker to pursue a more expansive ideal of salvation than that offered by many denominational stances. One of the greatest hazards of unthinking orthodoxy is complacency, that all the truth is contained in the particular denominational dogma and that there is no need to seek further. Indeed, this complacency may attain such a stranglehold that any conflicting data are, without any further ado, attributed to the devil with his powerful impersonating capacities. Only as the mind expands in love to consider other possibilities, can the traveller proceed along the spiritual path. In other words, complacency leads one to a prolonged halt, and the present situation is naively thought to be the end of the trail.

The psychic diversion with its gnostic affinities is an important distraction, especially as the path lengthens: the way of knowledge cannot be by-passed; on the contrary, it has to be embraced and made spiritual by the power of love. Condemnatory attitudes with paroxysms of zealous persecution, whether by religious authorities or the secular arm of the state, serve only to drive the gnostic faction underground, but in due course it always emerges, if anything strengthened by the harassment that it has been obliged to undergo, together with the martyrdom that so often accompanies it. In other words, ideas cannot be killed, even if their sponsors lie cold in the dust. This observation provides an ironical twist to St Paul's words of encouragement, 'Though our outer humanity is in decay, yet day by day we are inwardly renewed' (2 Corinthians 4.16). The ideal of total destruction has to be replaced by one of total redemption and resurrection. The same view is true also of advances in scientific understanding and the technology that arises from them. Mankind has been put in a position of power that even a few decades ago would have seemed visionary. How this power is used will determine the fate not only of the human species but also that of our entire planet. But the clock cannot be put back. We have to learn to work with our newly discovered knowledge so that it becomes a beneficial servant and not a Frankenstein's monster. The catalyst is love, and this comes from God alone.

The real knowledge comes from the unitive experience of God; the world's great saints and mystics have been given the key to that knowledge, and it is in turn their burden as well as their privilege to impart it to their fellow creatures. Like Moses, they have to construct their earthly work to the design shown them on the mountain of illumination. Once we can appreciate and follow the teaching of Christ, 'Set your mind on God's kingdom and his justice before everything else, and all the rest will come to you as well' (Matthew 6.33), we begin to grasp the truth, that contemplative prayer is the way of the path, not acquisitive knowledge whether scientific or occult. But as we proceed, such amazing understanding of the fabric of the universe, material and psychic, will be declared to us that we will scarcely be able to contain ourselves for joy that the creation is as it is. Again, as in the story of the Fall, it is our priorities that matter, to say nothing of our inner attitudes of humility and trust. Once we are ready, God does not withhold anything from our grasp. And the measure of our readiness to receive suprarational knowledge is our capacity to flow out in love to our neighbour.

A final thought seems not out of place. In the Parable of Dives and Lazarus (Luke 16.19-31), the chastened rich man in hell is told that if his five brothers will not listen to the teachings of Moses and the prophets, they will not be convinced of the terror in store for them after they die even if someone should rise from the dead to warn them. Charles Dickens, in his *A Christmas Carol*, seems to have taken a less pessimistic view: the ghost of his partner Marley comes to Ebenezer Scrooge in a dream and reveals the terrible consequences of the selfish, heartless life he, like Scrooge, had led while on earth. Scrooge is shaken out of his obduracy, and behaves for the first time in his life with charity to his employee Bob Cratchit and his family. Love enters his heart, no longer of stone but now of flesh, as he joins the little family circle for their humble Christmas meal.

Of course, both episodes belong to the world of fiction, but they can still be useful in our thinking. Thus a psychical event can serve to shatter the intellectual arrogance of a materialistic atheist, opening up his quaking mind to possibilities of existence previously out of the range of his conception. Then the receptive mind can go back to Moses and the prophets and start to learn the principles of the good life. Most of us need a strong jolt before we are prepared to move from our present point of view and explore new possibilities. The phenomena of spiritualism are usually crude and seldom impressive to the detached observer, but every now and then they may produce effects that change the life of a previously hardened sceptic. God does indeed work in mysterious ways, and we dare not limit the range of the Holy Spirit's activities. It must, of course, be acknowledged that the Bible, especially the Old Testament, contains numerous prohibitions against dabbling in occult matters, especially trafficking in communication with the deceased, and this is surely sound teaching, because the terrain is treacherous and the end-product inconclusive of the divine reality. But if some of us are endowed with special psychic powers as part of the inscrutable variations of personality that make us all individuals in our own right, so that we each have a unique contribution to make to the whole of the community, it seems inevitable that God expects us to use them. Here the Parable of the Talents seems especially pertinent: we have to use our gifts in the world and not bury them in obscurity. The question is always the same: what is the overriding motive? If it is for self-advancement there will be an ultimate fall, but if it is to God's greater glory and the benefit of our fellow creatures, there will be a final blessing, hard as the path may be. So long as we see all gifts, whether intellectual, artistic or psychic — to say nothing of material gifts of money, beauty and physical prowess — in this light, we will come to no harm.

I personally have no doubt that some of us are given shafts of light quite unpredictably into the future as well as the life of the world to come. They are, in my opinion, not to be eschewed as the work of the devil any more than dismissed as aberrant workings of the mind. They are, on the contrary, to be hailed as a special grace from God, and often they may be of help to someone in our vicinity who is desperately depressed or bereaved. But the gift is not to be sought for its own sake. It is to be handed back to God for his purposes as we proceed quietly along the path in contemplative awareness of the present moment.

8 The Dark Light of Faith

The work continues, the journey to the pearl of great price proceeds beyond the diversions of visions, communications and gnostic speculations intriguing as all these are, and none without some substance of truth. Yet at their most impressive they are merely commentaries of the way, culled from those who have proceeded further and who may well, in the life beyond death, have learned to jettison much of the teaching as merely compendious and of little real help. We may in this respect remember the Rich Young Man who approached Jesus, asking what he had to do in order to attain eternal life. He had followed the moral code of the Ten Commandments but still had not attained the inner rest that is the criterion of truly spiritual illumination. His heart remained restless, being only too aware that the pearl was at present outside his grasp, despite all his good intentions. Jesus told him to sell his possessions and give the proceeds to the poor, and then he should follow him, but the renunciation demanded was too great for the young man, who left in sorrow.

This episode is usually taken as a rebuke against wealth; it is easier for the camel to pass through the eye of a needle than for a rich man to enter heaven. But the matter is less simple than this. Money is important: did not St Paul make a collection from his various gentile churches to help the mother congregation at Jerusalem? Clearly Jesus divined in this particular instance that the person was too dependent on material things, and that until he had left them behind him, there was no possibility of his entering the gate of life. He could just as easily have been a scholar intoxicated with his great learning, an artist enamoured with his talent or an athlete wedded to his physical prowess. In each instance, the person would devote himself sedulously to the cultivation of his private riches, and in the process of self-development, he would shut himself off from the world's greater need; yet his very proficiency, if properly directed, could in one way or another add its quota to serving the world.

71

To what we are attached becomes our prison; what we possess in our own soul is our domain of freedom. It is in this spirit that the first Beatitude finds its full expression: blessed are the poor in spirit (those who know their need of God), for the kingdom of heaven is theirs (Matthew 5.3). It should be noted that this is not a promise of future bliss, but a statement of present reality. To know one's need of God is to be in the divine courtyard. When one knocks at the door in resolute conviction, one is admitted. But the entrance to the kingdom is less immediately satisfying than one might have expected. Indeed, every expectation has to be surrendered before the fullness of God's grace is vouchsafed one. And all this is an aspect of the darkness of faith. The harder one seeks for assurances the less satisfied does one become. All this is pertinent to the dilemma of the Rich Young Man who was told that God alone is good and that the things of the world are vain in the face of the divine reality.

The early assurance that God is real, the spiritual path the only one that counts, that there is a deeper meaning to each event in our lives, that the highest values are the surest guides to a fulfilled life, is gradually dulled as we tread in the way of common existence. All those around us are led by the concerns of immediate survival and the diversions from work that serve as enjoyments. Entertainments would be a sounder description. We speak about people enjoying themselves, when they can indulge in some special pleasure, but in fact such activity is really an escape from the self into a world of fantasy and diversion, not necessarily bad in itself but essentially trivial and inconsequential. To enjoy oneself ought to mean precisely that: to revel in one's own being and marvel at the creativity of God as made manifest in one's own mind and body. We have already considered the amazed delight of the biblical writer who marvels at the creation of humanity in Psalm 8. This is the joy in oneself that is the true measure of glorified humanity. Yet we lose contact with our own divine humanity in the cut and thrust of mundane existence. The pearl is eased out of sight by the things around us, rather like the seed being choked by the thistles, the vision being clouded over by worldly cares and the false glamour of wealth.

Wealth in this context has once more a wider spectrum than mere material riches. It is the complacent assumption of the worldly-wise that a surface view of life, in which matter is the only landmark, is the total of reality. To them spiritual aspirations are vain, pathetic attempts to escape from the facts of life, its transience and the finality of death; spiritual ideas are conjured up by the imagination to make existence more tolerable. So they would tell us, and, of course, like so many dogmatic statements with provocative overtones, these contain sufficient truth to make the seeker flinch. A faith that cannot face destructive criticism is like a house built on sand. Only an honest agnosticism can provide the rock on which a house may safely stand and confront the hostile elements around it. We see 'through a glass darkly', glimpsing only puzzling reflections in a mirror, as St Paul puts it in 1 Corinthians 13.12, but in the fullness of time we shall see face to face. As we grope, so we attain the courage to go on. It is faith that leads us on to the clearer vision of truth, but while we are alive in the flesh, the clarity of vision will remain imperfect. In the famous definition of Hebrews 11.1, faith gives substance to our hopes and makes us certain of realities that we do not see. But the certainty can mislead us as well as guide us to truth. A blind faith can easily degenerate into credulity on the one hand and fanaticism on the other. Of course, a totally submissive faith is sometimes essential in a time of crisis when we cannot do other than trust in those around us and leave ourselves completely open to the divine providence. Thus a patient has perforce to trust in the skill of his surgeon or dentist when he abdicates his judgement to their control, whether in normal consciousness or under general anaesthesia. But the control is only temporary, and when it is relaxed, the individual's free will is restored.

This rather trite example shows us both the value of faith and its dangers. A situation can arise in which people find themselves under the domination of a demonic master-figure whom they accept as an infallible guide, obeying his commands with the alacrity of willing slaves and being led in the direction of destruction with wanton abandon; our own century has seen too many examples of dictators and demagogues for our comfort, and the same applies in the history of religious faith, including Christianity. The faith in an institution, a theological stance, or even the Bible or the sacraments of the Church can easily supplant the total faith in God by which alone we are saved. There is a terrible irony in all this, for the basis of Christian understanding is a living faith in God as manifested in the ministry of his incarnate Son Jesus Christ, who atoned for the world's sin by his sacrificial death on the cross of human cruelty. The transaction involved in the atonement, basic as it is to Christian doctrine, is seldom adequately explained in terms of dogmatic theology, so that the Father is not made to appear a vengeful potentate who needs in some way to be satisfied or propitiated. Then alone may his wrath by assuaged sufficiently for him to forgive human sinfulness and a new covenant made possible. In fact, it is in the course of life that we begin to grasp inwardly how Christ acted as a substitute — and indeed always acts in this way — so that the immensity of human sin might be taken up by him and presented to the Father for gracious reception and unconditional healing. By Christ we are reconciled to God in love, and our burden of guilt is lifted from us. But the price to be paid, the penance that follows the absolution, is an amendment of life. This amendment means a changed style of living in which we are subject to the divine obedience and no longer the dictates of the flesh. The essential divine commandment is love, and this involves the willingness to give up everything one has to succour even the lowest creature. In this we do not forget that we ourselves are that lowest creature, like the publican in Jesus' Parable of the Publican and the Pharisee (Luke 18.9-14). This love is no sentimental outpouring of ourselves in a moment of guilt for our past misdemeanours. It is a commitment to bring the world to that knowledge of the sacrifice of Christ by enacting it, however inadequately, in our own lives. It is stern and fearsome as well as warm and welcoming: after the warm welcome comes the directive to spiritual living, 'There must be no bounds to your goodness, as your heavenly Father's goodness knows no bounds' (Matthew 5.48).

To return to the classical definition of faith in the Letter to the Hebrews, the certainty of realities we do not see that faith guarantees is brought about, not by wishful thinking, but by action. Even when the mirror of life shows only puzzling reflections, we have to proceed onwards as the way opens. It may be a way through a wilderness of banal trivialities of the common round, severe physical disablement, the uncertainties of artistic creativeness, or service in defence of society by armed strength. In all these different paths the end is the same: the slow ascent of the mountain of transfiguration where the full Christ reveals himself. But such a movement and belief are objects of faith, not reason. In the end the human lives in a realm of spiritual values, without which he descends to his physical status as the most intelligent, and therefore potentially the most destructive, of all the animal creation. A good working definition of faith is 'the resolution to stand and fall by the noblest hypothesis'. This was propounded by Frederic Myers who lived in the nineteenth century and was a scholar, a poet of some distinction, and one of the founding fathers of the Society for Psychical Research. This subject even today evokes the most acrimoniously hostile reactions among many scientists and Christians: the former deny its validity as a discipline, while the latter associate it with workings of demonic agencies. In the instance of Myers, the noble hypothesis was the rectitude of investigating psychical phenomena in the light of truth, an ideal that should inspire all scientific research.

In the Platonic triad of virtues that lead the intellect up to the vision of God there are beauty, truth and goodness (or love in the Christian context). That any of these three great qualities does in fact have such a destination is a matter of pure faith, for in the world it seems so often that the powers of darkness hold sway. Ugliness, deceit and cruelty govern the lives of so many people both as individuals and as members of a tainted society. The prince of lies certainly seems to gain spectacular victories, at least in the short term. Unfortunately this 'short term' may embrace the entire span of many people's lives. Indeed, the prevalence of evil, especially its manifest triumph in many situations, is one of the hardest problems for those who believe in divine providence. It may be, as the writer of Psalm 73 declares, that the end of the evil doer is not a pleasant one — for he puts himself out of fellowship with all the world around him — but that the injured and persecuted gain ultimate justice and attain peace is still unproven in terms of a future state of being. We begin to learn, however, that peace is something that has to grow in us now rather than merely be a condition that we may anticipate at the end of our lives, when we enter into a hoped-for greater existence after death. The first type of peace is an experience of reality at the present moment, whereas the second type is a deeply longed-for release that is underlined by faith. Nevertheless it is not unreasonable to project a present experience into the future, whereas the expectation of something quite different from what we now know is an act of faith that borders on a dangerous credulity. As Jesus tells Nicodemus, 'In very truth I tell you, we speak of what we know and testify to what we have seen, and you reject our testimony' (John 3.11). Experience alone confirms that testimony.

The spur to faith is the intimation of glory with which we started this account, the pearl seen at a great distance from us in heavenly vision. As the path is trudged in weariness of soul, so the vision is clouded over to the point of extinction by the affairs of the world and the barren disbelief that emanates from our fellows. The great test is to proceed onwards, despite the destructive chorus of disbelief, ridicule and disillusion around us. The unresolved problem of evil triumphing over the will to good, already alluded to, has to be accepted as a fact of life. The arguments inherent in theodicy, the justification of divine providence in the face of evil, have to be both heard with the outer ear and transcended by the inner one. To become engrossed in intellectual speculations only brings us back to the assertive realm of gnosis. It is highly diverting but of limited practical value, since the ways of God are immeasurably higher than those of man. We grope in our suffering and then the veil is momentarily lifted so that we can see in a flash the vast expanse ahead of us, threatening and consoling at the same time. It threatens because of its vastness; consoles because of the divine presence at the heart of all creation. This does not mean that the reasoning faculty is left behind, but rather that it is put in abeyance until sufficient data are available from one's own experience to fashion a new metaphysic. This in turn will certainly be refashioned on more than one occasion as fresh insights come to one.

On one occasion when the teaching of Jesus seemed so outrageous in its claims of personal transcendence that many would-be followers left him, he cast his eyes on his own little flock and asked them whether they too wanted to depart. The reply of Peter is very touching, 'Lord, to whom shall we go? Your words are words of eternal life. We have faith, and we know that you are the Holy One of God' (John 6.68-69). The faith that Peter proclaimed then, and at parallel passages in the Synoptic Gospels, was to be tested almost beyond endurance when the man he called the Holy One of God was divested of all his power and authority, submitting meekly to the process of the civil and religious law governed by vicious, fearful administrators. On one occasion he was to deny knowledge of Jesus on three consecutive occasions, thereby saving his skin but lacerating his inner integrity. And yet, had the skin not been saved, Peter would have died a martyr's death long before the appointed time, since he was to have an extended period of ministry ahead of him. The darkness of faith may lead us into some strange situations and some bizarre encounters with the most unlikely people, but we have to forge our way ahead. The essential saving quality of the cowardly Peter was his persistence; unlike Judas Iscariot, he had the humility to press onwards despite his lacerated soul and tremulous body. His remorse led not to suicide but to a chastening of the soul so that he could understand the weakness of his fellow creatures. It is of interest that Peter's faith in God's providence did not burgeon to full flower for a long time after the pentecostal experience. Thus we read in Galatians 2.11-14 how he and some other Christian leaders refused to eat with gentile converts in the presence of Jewish Christians, an attitude completely at variance with the basic teaching of the faith and his own prior joyful reception of Cornelius and his family into it. It is very hard to walk the steady path of faith when so many temptations beset us: fear of being placed outside the pale, concern for our worldly reputation, a desire not to offend others lest they in turn reject us. In terms of the quest for the pearl of integrity how trivial are all these considerations! We can in this light see even more clearly the temptations in front of the Rich Young Man that barred his entrance to the kingdom of heaven.

The essence of the faith that leads us on the path to God is the capacity to renounce a present assurance for the hard, rugged contours of the future promise. In the instance of Job all outer landmarks of simple identity had to be shed — wealth, reputation, family ties, health — before the futile theological discussion with his friends ended on a note of silent ignorance. Then God showed himself — a presence involved in the whole creation and not only Job's welfare. It could well be that God is available to reveal himself to all of us, but only the radical renunciation of all beloved personal possessions can leave us open and ready to receive the divine guest who is also the eternal host at the heavenly banquet. The essential ingredient of a growing faith is a sturdy undercurrent of doubt. If faith leads us onwards in the visionary journey to the pearl, doubt anchors us firmly on the solid ground where we have to conduct our daily affairs, mixing with various types of people and learning in the school of life with its constant change and disconcerting transience. Perhaps the hardest renunciation on the tortuous road of faith is faith itself. By this I allude to a dogmatic religious conviction that is well anchored in the security of a long tradition. How often is the recent convert absolutely sure of the fundamental principles of his newly found religious faith! He may excel even the leaders of that religious denomination in his punctilious observance and enthusiastic statement of belief. It is for this reason that religious converts — and these include devotees of Marx, Freud and others of an atheistic frame of mind — are frequently difficult to know, let alone willing to debate matters pertaining to their belief. In fact, they are often highly insecure people who need a firm structure of dogma for their emotional support. This in itself is no bad thing in the early stages of a religious pilgrimage, but in due course it is essential for the seeker after truth to come to terms with the less acceptable, more questionable tenets of his new faith, and also the invariable fact that the lives and actions of religious groups tend often lamentably to belie their depth of belief. In other words there is often a wide gulf between orthodoxy and orthopraxis. The type of faith that is open and can give credit to others of different traditions is by far the healthiest. By contrast, an enclosed dogmatic belief system tends to imprison its adherents in a mental structure that permits of little exploration outside its own limits. It induces a feeling of complacent security but allows little growth. It is sad but seemingly inevitable that this type of system claims the largest number of adherents, whereas the open, tolerant way appeals only to the few who can think and decide for themselves. Where there is inner strength, there need be no fear of outside contamination. Where there is inner insecurity, there is the greatest fear of outside subversion. The end of all this can be savage persecution of those who are deemed to be heretics. These always challenge the belief of the masses, who derive strength from dogma rather than from God.

It is a moment of great release when we can admit that we do not know the answers to the world's many problems, that even the course of our lives over the next few days is completely hidden from us, that we cannot control the future events in store for us let alone those of our immediate circle of family and friends. This realization is in fact a product of age and experience, and is one of the most delicious fruits of the autumn of life. Then we can grasp the meaning of the celebrated tenth verse of Psalm 46: 'be still and know that I am God'. This psalm tells us that although terrible cosmic disasters may threaten the world and great wars endanger the very citadel of God's temple, we should have faith in the omnipotence of God and rest in his power. Indeed, in any situation of calamity the most useful helpers are those who can remain calm. Their very presence is balm in its own right, and furthermore their particular skills will be most effectively used in the moment of need. It is an interesting paradox that the person who can call on the name of the Lord in an extremity will be able to act far more usefully than the one who believes that he alone can do anything, and therefore becomes increasingly tense with anxiety. His officiousness is more likely to disturb those around him than assist them in their work.

All this, of course, can easily degenerate into the notorious mystical heresy of quietism, in which the impetus for action is laid at God's door, while we do nothing except in response to the divine initiative. Apart from the abdication of human responsibility, a consequence of the free will given us, that such an attitude would engender, we might all too easily misinterpret the divine command, or worse still be misled by a counterfeit instruction issued by some psychic agency in the intermediate dimension. Quietism is the antithesis of activism, which has already been alluded to, in which we believe that only our own actions can help, and therefore become obsessively involved in good works of various types. Unfortunately our innate egoism intrudes, and soon personal conflict follows as each pursues his own way. The story of the Tower of Babel

(Genesis 11.1-9) is a parable of activism: God is excluded and the work disintegrates in conflict, so that the common language of love that binds all creation together is confused and each group retires to its own stronghold as a separate entity in mistrust of the others.

The true faith is a trust in the love of God, which Christians would see demonstrated in the death and resurrection of Jesus Christ. In that faith we can rest in the divine providence in prayer, and the strength imparted to us by the Holy Spirit will help to integrate our own gifts for the work ahead, whether it be the routine of the common round or a sudden emergency that could not reasonably have been anticipated. In this frame of mind we can work in collaboration with God in the ceaseless creation of the world. As Psalm 127 reminds us, unless the Lord builds the house, its builders will have toiled in vain. But we have to put the divine plan into concrete form, like Moses on Mount Sinai being told by God to work to the design which he was shown on the mountain. This is true reconciliation of the extremes of quietism and activism. Another way of seeing this is the relationship between good works and faith. St Paul states categorically that we are saved by God's gift of grace and not by our own efforts, so that we have nothing to boast of. St James, on the other hand, reminds us that faith, if it does not lead to action, is in itself a lifeless thing (James 2.17). Faith in fact is proved by action; this is the great difference between faith and belief, which itself is merely a detached mental attitude. But once it takes flesh, it becomes a living faith which may even change the course of history as it did in the apostolic era of Christianity. It is energized by a driving force that will, at least metaphorically, move mountains. This was the work of the prophets of Israel, notably Jeremiah who could no more resist the impulse to speak the truth in God's name to his sinful compatriots than could the fictional Jonah evade his duty by fleeing to the ends of the earth.

Thus Frederic Myers' definition of faith as the resolution to stand and fall by the noblest hypothesis is made possible by the prior infusion of divine grace into us. Then we will stand up to all ridicule, persecution and ostracism even to the point of death, because to betray the truth would be a sin against the Holy Spirit himself. This would be tantamount to committing suicide, as did Judas Iscariot, and while I personally believe that all created things will be brought back to life by the love of God, the punishment in store for those who deny the truth is a severe one: the inability to look themselves in the face. The hardest thing in the world is to forgive ourselves; until we are open to the love of God it is in fact impossible, because our pride excludes us from the greater fellowship of life.

9   The Still Point

In us alone is stillness. All outside is chaos and confusion. T. S. Eliot, in *Burnt Norton*, writes of the still point of the turning world. The moment at hand is the fulcrum of the lever, the axle of the wheel. Our inner peace resonates with the peace of God known in the point of time which is the present moment, and then we effect communion with all that lives. When we know that peace and can call upon it at any time, the pearl of great price is not very far from our grasp because the acquisition of that peace entails the renunciation of all we possess. Then alone can we be so naked of self-regard as to pass through the needle's eye into the kingdom of heaven. So St Paul can write with complete self-knowledge.

> We wield the weapons of righteousness in right hand and left. Honour and dishonour, praise and blame are alike our lot; we are the impostors who speak the truth, the unknown men whom all men know; dying we still live on; disciplined by suffering, we are not done to death; in our sorrows we have always cause for joy; poor ourselves, we bring wealth to many; penniless, we own the world (2 Corinthians 6.7-10).

St Paul attained this state of blessed equanimity by being continually about his Father's business in the presence of the Lord Jesus, no matter what he was doing or what people he was addressing. He was all things to all men, not by sacrificing his own unique personality and trying to merge imperceptibly into the present company, but by being so open in love that the other person could find his rest in him. This is, in fact, the secret of spiritual direction, as it is of spiritual healing. When we get out of the way in humble service, God can get in and so renew our mind that we can be what is right to the person with whom we are dealing.

To evacuate our inner castle so that God may enter is, paradoxically, to take full charge of our own domain. The situation is very different from leaving ourselves wide open, through unwise meditation exercises or occult practices — to say nothing of the use of drugs that dull the mind — to the indeterminate psychic forces around us. The essence of this inner submission to God is the act of prayer, and a consideration of this essential spiritual practice is important in the path ahead of us. In prayer the mind ascends to God by its own action yet effected by grace. It is God who prays through us quite as much as we who pray to God; the relationship is reciprocal. Dame Julian of Norwich was shown that 'God is the ground of our beseeching', the foundation of our praying, and St Paul states (in Romans 8.26-8) that we do not know how we even ought to pray, but through our inarticulate groans the Spirit himself is pleading for us, and God who searches our innermost being knows what the Spirit means, because he pleads for God's people in God's own way, and as we know, all things work together for good for those who love God. The impetus to pray comes from us, but the need is awakened from within for we can never be completely at rest in ourselves until we know the divine presence. It may be a Prodigal-Son-type of experience that brings home to us the truth of this, but as we ascend the spiritual path, so prayer becomes as vital to the soul as does air to the body.

The great action of prayer is to be still, and this in turn requires an attitude of faith that there is a presence who knows one's heart and hears the inner depths of one's need. This is the other side of the admonition to be still and know that I am God. If we are still in wordless devotion to all that lives, we will know the presence of God, the knowledge of unitive love between creature and Creator. This unitive knowledge is the ultimate relationship; while intellectual knowledge separates the know-er from the thing known, inasmuch as what is known hence-forth becomes an object to be used and manipulated, unitive knowledge, by contrast, brings the subject and object together so that a new creature is conceived and a new life begun. Each loses itself in order to find its true nature. To be sure, God can never lose himself, but his courtesy is such that he gives of himself in so humble a fashion that he can be grasped by even the lowliest creature.

If we seek God acquisitively, as we have already noted, we remain empty of the divine presence because the unhappy, grasping ego is in charge and will not move from its place of authority; and so, in the silence of contemplation, the work of faith is simply to be aware of the present moment with overtones of thankfulness that we are in a situation in which we can be quiet without disturbance (in many countries this basic privacy is impossible to obtain either because of the overcrowding of poverty or the intrusion of an inimical political state that seeks to crush the religion of the spirit). The silence is its own reward; we are not to look for any 'sign' of God's presence, but as we grow in faith, so we will be increasingly aware of the wordless dialogue proceeding deep within us. This is the silent conversation with God that warms the heart and mobilizes the powers of the mind and spirit with which we are all endowed, but which largely remain in abeyance in everyday life, until we are enabled to strike a deeper note of awareness. In other words, the effect of God's grace shows itself as we give of ourselves unsparingly moment by moment. We suddenly are amazed by what we are given, but, far from dwelling on it, we stride forward in resolution to give what we have to those around us.

God is the foundation of our praying, and as we are still before his ineffable presence, so we spontaneously address him either in word or in thought. In fact our conversation is a response to his presence and the inner knowledge he gives us about our own state of moral and spiritual poverty. He knows all, but it is important that we too should know it: the prayer of petition and confession brings to us an intimate understanding of what we really lack and of our need of inner cleansing. Our problems over relationships, whether in the family or at work, provoke in their turn an understanding of our own deficiencies that have precipitated these difficulties. In fact we cannot change other people according to our will; all we can hope for is a change in ourselves; then the new radiance within us may indeed influence others to become less defensive and more open to love. In the end it is love alone that can effect a permanent change in a person; by contrast, coercion, no matter how subtly it is applied, evokes a deeper resentment that will find its own destructive expression in due course. This applies equally to hellfire religion, intellectual brilliance that wins the debate, or fulsome flattery that moves the person in the direction marked out by his subversive adversary.

In the work of continuous creation of the world the human and the divine act, at least ideally, in peaceful co-operation. The essence of prayer is intimate fellowship of the person with God, while the effect of prayer is the infusion of the person with the power of the Holy Spirit. This Spirit not only renews the personality and sets in motion a sequence of cleansing and healing of all that is awry, but is also transmitted to others in the act of intercession. When we are quiet before God in childlike faith and remember a person in need in loving solicitude, it seems that the power of the Spirit of God flows directly to that person. If he is receptive, he will be strengthened by the Holy Spirit, and in some measure enabled to attain a healing. Even if a physical malady cannot honestly be said to show any manifest improvement, there will be an inner strengthening of resolve, accompanied by a calming of distraught emotions, and an infusion of radiant hope that will lead the one who is ill onwards to full recovery. Where the progress is clearly in the direction of the death we all have in our own time to experience, a blessing of peace will descend on the dying person and his sorrowing relatives that will somehow guide both of them in the way ahead, whether in this life or the life beyond death. The heart of prayer is warm silence and trustful tranquillity, in the presence of which radical changes are set in motion in the personality of the one who is praying and in those for whom he prays. Furthermore, earnest prayer radiates far beyond the person for whom intercession is offered; it can also influence those far off and play its quiet part in changing the attitudes and widening the perspectives of world leaders and the celebrities who exert so powerful an influence on the crowds and especially the young. Indeed, if peace is finally to descend on our war-torn world, it can do so only by the radiant love that follows communion with God. He makes no outer demands, but somehow effects a change in us so that we can serve our neighbour in outflowing devotion.

Prayer is the energizing act of the soul, to be carried out in the first instance at set times and places but eventually at all times and everywhere. The fellowship with God renews our strength and directs our awareness to the things of ultimate value, of final importance. In the divine presence it becomes increasingly difficult to behave deceitfully or without consideration for others. This is not because a distant God is watching us, threatening us with punishment if we persist in our evil ways. It is, on the contrary, the divine presence within us that will be content with nothing less than a return to the source which is both its origin and destination. But when it does return home, it will have brought the individual personality with it, and the work performed by the person, small as it may appear to those who believe they are further on the way to sanctification, will be his particular gift to God. The resolution and sacrifice come from the human agent, but the inner strength is of divine origin. In this frame of mind sin gradually recedes, and in its place there appears a radiant loving service, an imprint of the divine image of which the seed has alone survived in the rat-race of common life. Our gift to God is our transformed personality, which shows itself in a deepened devotion to our fellows and a mature responsibility to the creation around us. These all have to be brought back to the Creator with our special stamp of identity attached to them — an identity at once personal and universal, inasmuch as it is now no longer the personal ego that is in command but the presence of Christ himself. This presence does not take over the personal identity or even overshadow it; it simply cleanses and heals it, so that, for the first time in its conscious existence, it can reveal the person clearly and with radiance. If only people could be disembarrassed of the accretion of worldly corruption that clings to them, they would be seen in their pristine radiance! Love then would indeed banish fear, for there is a great beauty in the healed human form, which is also that of the little child we have to become before we can enter the kingdom of heaven.

The still point is known and that knowledge cultivated by the constant practice of contemplative prayer. But at the same time the peace of the still point of stability in the roaring vortex of worldly activity is constantly borne down upon and threatened by that activity with its undertones of anxious hurry and impatience. This is a crucially important part of the development of the still point and its gift to the world. There can be no effective journey on the path to the pearl of great price, until we are so inwardly poised that our attention and resolution remain in control even when the world is collapsing around us. In other words, real prayer never ceases. The intensive periods of contemplation with their developments of petition, confession and intercession may come to an end, but the atmosphere of prayer remains with us as we come down to earth and pursue our daily work. We operate decisively from the still point within: it is in fact the divine presence. This knowledge is unitive, binding us to the ineffable Creator and also to his creation, especially our fellow humans. Its fruits are the classical harvest of the Holy Spirit: love, joy, peace, patience, kindness, goodness, fidelity, gentleness and self-control, as enumerated so memorably by St Paul in Galatians 5.22. None of these can be simulated or even developed by an act of will, because the ego has to be displaced from its customary seat of domination before we can receive them. They are all a free gift of God, but until we operate from the still point within us, they will be dissipated amid the hectic turmoil of the chaos around us. That point of inner rest is not far from the source of the pearl, and the occupation of the point may cost us everything we own. This is a part of the selling all we have to purchase the pearl.

On an outer level the work from the point shows itself in unhurried harmony with the world around us, especially the jarring note of those who are emotionally disturbed. One imagines Jesus going forth on his healing ministry, which included the morally sick tax-gatherers, prostitutes, drunkards and others, no less than the physically disabled: he came as doctor to the sick, not to the healthy, but, alas, there was little health in any of his fellows. The obviously sick in body and mind, being aware of their need of healing, were actually closer to health than were those who prided themselves on their moral excellence. They did not know that this was merely an outer facade that hid a well of corruption inside themselves. It seems to me that when Jesus visited company of a low order in response to their invitation to share their conviviality, he arrived in a state of inner calm and outer benevolence that showed itself as a presence that could heal all those open to him. I cannot imagine him either judging the company or preaching at them to renounce their evil ways. If this had been his style, he would not have been welcome in such quarters.

On one occasion, noted at the beginning of the fifteenth chapter of Luke's Gospel, various bad characters, including the despised tax-gatherers who collaborated with the loathed Roman occupying power and no doubt practised extortion on their brethren, crowded around Jesus to listen to him, much to the disapproval of the respectable religious authorities. He had that inner peace that could speak to all who had ears to hear; he needed neither coercion with hellfire threats nor the offensive condescension so often unconsciously poured out by the insensitive almsgiver on those he seeks to assist. Had Jesus been either a preacher of doom or a well-meaning philanthropist, he would have evoked scorn and aversion among his erring audience. The outcasts of society, by virtue of their very dereliction, can usually see through cant and hypocrisy more readily than their privileged, affluent fellows. Their native self-esteem, often wrongly equated with pride, would soon reject overtures from any except the true bearer of love. It seems clear to me that Jesus was essentially quiet during the festivities of such people. He neither judged them nor did he try to ingratiate himself with them by adopting their turn of speech, manner or general life-style. But his presence with its outflowing radiance filled his hosts with an unwonted love that set in motion a change in their moral perspective. That presence acted as a clear mirror in which they could see themselves. His acceptance affirmed their importance as people in their own right, while the reflected image showed how tarnished they were, how the divine image was encrusted with layers of filth. Nevertheless, the promise of healing was extended to all who could accept the current situation and move towards a new way of life. This seems to have been the great difference between the harsh denunciation of St John Baptist and the gentle invitation of Jesus. In fact both were necessary: the Baptist jolted his hearers out of their complacency, while Jesus could accept them for what they were in order to direct them to what they were meant to become. These are the two motions of love: acceptance and direction. Without the first there is no contact, without the second no movement. From the still point Jesus could flow out to his audience in a service of love unadulterated by emotional outbursts or threatening displays of anger. And so he could gradually lead them like a shepherd of his flock to the pastures of fulfilment where they could be gods in their own right. A god in this context is a focus of free will, one that can respond positively to outside and interior stimuli rather than simply being driven by them like an animal in front of its overseer. God can work with the god-like person, created in his own image, for the continuous creation of the world to its time of resurrection into eternal life.

The test of our inner stillness is its maintenance during the heavy excursions of daily life. Does the spiritual aspirant move beyond destruction emotions, such as anxiety, fear, anger and resentment? The sad but true answer is 'No'. On the contrary, these destructive states of mind assail us more insistently than before as we proceed on our journey towards acquiring the precious pearl. The hard carapace of worldly indifference is stripped from us and our psychic vulnerability becomes exquisitely apparent both to us and those around us. The vulnerability is not only to the unhealed depths within us, but also to the harsh currents of the outside world. Were this not the case we would not grow spiritually, neither could we play our part in healing the world's distress. It is no surprise that the Holy Spirit leads Jesus directly into the field of dark temptation when he has accepted the enigmatic baptism of repentence from John — enigmatic inasmuch as he in himself is without stain. But in a strange way, by submitting to that humiliation he plays his part in repenting for the pain of suffering inherent in creation. Of this he is indeed the ultimate source, inasmuch as all things were made by him as the Son of the Father, the Lamb of God slain from the foundation of the world in the form of those who have suffered in the cause of righteousness. But just as Jesus was protected inwardly by his divine power, so also can we call upon that power when we are floundering in the destructive psychic currents playing around us. This is a particularly valuable fruit of prayer: be still and enter the interior castle at the point of the heart, or better still, the centre of the abdomen, which normally is especially receptive to negative emotions. When that stillness has been registered, we become aware of a strength within us that gives us peace and encouragement. It tells us incontestably in wordless communication to let go of our particular problem and flow directly into the stream of the power. This is the still centre of our personal turning world, and when it is occupied without trepidation but in faith, a powerful love lifts up the heart and illuminates the psychic atmosphere around us. In other words, the still point is a centre of immense power, the power in fact of the Holy Spirit who is the gracious giver of life. In that power we can rest in assurance, knowing that we are protected even in the height of conflict around us.

To come to that still point is a major objective of the spiritual life. The uninformed may believe that this objective can be attained much more directly and less laboriously by a simple meditation technique, such as repeating a simple phrase or even a single word until the conscious whirling mind is stilled by a blanket of calm restfulness. But although such a method may indeed tap the resources of the centre temporarily, there will be little growth of the person or attainment of constant strength in the face of adversity. For this deeper knowledge of peace there has to be a confrontation with the whole inner psychological life and its spiritual basis in accordance with the principles we have already discussed earlier on in our consideration of the path to the precious pearl. Just as it cannot be snatched by the gnosis afforded by esoteric investigations and occult procedures, so it cannot be blandly appropriated by a meditation exercise. The whole pysche has to be cleansed and renovated, and this entails a wounding self-knowledge that will be content with nothing less than the truth of one's situation both in the world and in the depths of the soul. There are no short cuts to the summit of the mountain of transfiguration but many enticing diversions, some of which run parallel to the main path so as to deceive the very elect. But they all come to a blind end. It is a variation on the theme of the wide gate that leads to perdition as the broad road that proceeds from it is assiduously traversed.

Do techniques of stilling the mind have any place in the spiritual path? The answer is surely in the affirmative, provided the motivation is soundly based. There can be no condemnation against any legitimate means of self-development, whether physical, mental or spiritual; a healthy person is more useful to the community than one who functions below his best. But as soon as self-development becomes an end in itself, it attains a demonic power. It wars against possible rivals while entrapping the person himself in an ever-constricting web of self-concern. The technique becomes both an idol and a prison. But unfortunately we all have an infinite capacity for self-delusion. This is where membership of a group of fellow-seekers on the path is helpful, but the group must belong to a well-established tradition of spiritual authority and not a sect or cult that imprisons its adherents in the ideology of its organizers. The witness of a religious tradition of probity is the safeguard here. Though not infallible, it is at least illuminated by the lives and examples of its saints. When meditational techniques take place as a matter of course within a practising community of believers, they are invaluable in themselves and are balanced by earthly concerns of charity and worship in the larger community. The still point remains untried until its integrity is tested by the challenge of the noise and bustle of the multitudes around one. If we can remain calm and self-possessed amid the clamour of many voices, some of which are broadcasting conflicting views and contrary advice, we are near to our goal. The pearl is not far from us, waiting impatiently to be bought.

The well-known story, I believe of St Martin of Tours, is a good example of the truly still point. Legend has it that on one occasion, while deep in rapt prayer in his cell, he was visited by an angel. But just as the conversation was proceeding with his heavenly visitor, he was interrupted by the clamour of the crowds outside waiting for him to give them food in accordance with his celebrated charity. What should he do — stay in his cell or attend to the human need at the cost of relinquishing his angelic visitor in the depth of prayer? The saint with a heavy heart ministered to the people, but when he returned later to his cell he was amazed to see it illuminated by the presence of the angel. When he articulated his joyful astonishment that such a being should have patiently awaited his return, he was told, 'Had you not left me, I needs must have left you'. The angel was as close to the saint in the noisy streets of the city as he was in the sanctuary of his cell. St Martin had proved his sanctity by relinquishing private prayer for worldly action; in fact his prayer had been intensified thereby. On the other hand, had he dismissed the world's need in the quietness of his cell, he would at once have cut himself off from God.

It has been my experience that as my own prayer life has deepened, so I can tolerate interruption more easily and return to the silence of inner communion with God more rapidly. The telephone ceases to be an enemy that has to be disconnected during times of prayer, but can instead be promptly answered when a caller breaks into the silence. The call, nearly always one of importance and often of immediate need, seems frequently to intensify the subsequent silent period of intercession rather than disrupt it. From this experience I have learned how an immediate distraction to prayer can in the end be the spur to a much more fulfilled prayer life, tranquil, strong, and opening the very soul to God's presence. The love of our neighbour potentiates our communion with God. This communion fills us with even more love that overflows in grateful service. The still point of the turning world is something not merely for the aspirant to attain as a private landmark, but also to take into the world of ceaseless activity with him. Then he becomes a focus of calm, a glow of benediction, a radiant source of love, and evokes in his turn a changed consciousness of all around him. And so where once there was, in the phrasing of St Francis' famous prayer, hatred there is now love; injury, pardon; doubt, faith; despair, hope; darkness, light; sadness, joy. The person who flows out from the still point is indeed an instrument of God's peace.

10   *Aggravations*

The still point of the turning world is the deep centre of the soul, the spirit where the Spirit of God lies immanent, bringing us to an active rest where, in our peace, we may serve the world according to his will. The divine will unites with the free human will — unites, it will be noted, not fuses — so that the divine purpose may inform the human understanding, while the human experience of life as it is may direct the divine initiative along the most immediately profitable course of action. So we even in our most inspired moments have to 'make friends with the mammon of unrighteousness', make use of our worldly wealth (in all its aspects) to win friends for ourselves, as we have considered in the strange Parable of the Unjust Steward that introduces the sixteenth chapter of St Luke's Gospel. The worldly are indeed more astute than the other-worldly in dealing with their own kind; they at least can effect some relationship with the unpalatable realities of daily life and the people who throng the roads in search of comfort. By contrast, the other-worldly live largely in a world of their own imagining and, despite their good intentions, tend to elude actual contact with many of life's urgent problems. The imagination of pious people can contrive an existence that has little in common with the dangerous world we are called on to inhabit and exalt.

When we function from the spirit within, we are well protected, for the divine source strengthens us against adversity as we attain a firm balance amid the storm of confusion and violence raging around us. But such a close spiritual contact is at first evanescent, becoming a more settled part of our lives only by long apprenticeship in the school of everyday existence. It is made possible by a life of contemplative prayer; the word meditation is widely canvassed nowadays, but its zenith is a stillness in which we are one with the source of all being, whatever name that source may be given according to the tradition of the aspirant. But prayer is the ideal, not simply meditation, since the end of prayer is intercession for the whole world, whereas even the most regular meditation can become a mere personal indulgence. The experience of bliss remains a selfish end until that bliss is bestowed on the world, a challenge impossible until one has, like Christ, descended from the divine heights to the soiled human depths.

It is indeed the soiled human condition that breaks in on us continually as we trudge with laboured steps in the direction of the pearl. This condition is both personal and communal. Some of the personal hindrances to spiritual progress have already been mentioned, and in them the combination of honest awareness and the power of prayer can help to lighten the way. This enlightenment is a gradual process for, just as an eye in darkness has to accommodate itself slowly to the light of day, so the sluggish human psyche can imbibe only a limited amount of truth at any one time. As T. S. Eliot remarks, in *Burnt Norton*, 'Human kind cannot bear very much reality'. But as we enter more fully into the light of spiritual day, so do the disturbances of the world around us impinge more painfully upon our sacred silence, tempting us to respond in kind to the outer irritations. As we hit out, so do we lose our spiritual balance. Then at once we fall into the sea of discord around us, and forfeit, at least temporarily, our vision of the pearl set high above on the mountain of transfiguration.

It is in this frame of reference that we can begin to understand the shattering demands of Jesus:

> Do not set yourself against the man who wrongs you. If someone slaps you on the right cheek, turn and offer your left. If a man wants to sue you for your shirt, let him have your coat as well. If a man in authority makes you go one mile, go with him two. Give when you are asked to give; and do not turn your back on a man who wants to borrow (Matthew 5.39-42).

The more we become emotionally involved with our own rights and privileges, the more do we forfeit that holy equanimity on which all truly constructive action is founded. But this teaching is indeed hard: there is no magic key for the solution of any particular personal or communal problem. Jesus' teaching, if followed literally on every occasion of provocation, would lead to the invariable triumph of the strong over the weak, the dishonest over the humble seeker of justice. We have indeed to resist evil, but the principle of movement is inner acceptance, a less equivocal way than non-violent resistance, which is used for frank moral coercion in political fields. The political protagonist of non-violent resistance is often animated by hatred against his adversary, and this in turn evokes its own quota of hatred against the one who resists. As the Buddha taught at the beginning of the *Dhammapada*, 'Hatred never ceases by hatred; hatred ceases only by love: this is the eternal law.'

When therefore we are the object of a personal attack of the type alluded to by Jesus, instead of hitting out against our assailant or detractor at once without due reflection, we should return to the still point in complete confidence. There we will be in communion with the divine presence, and a deeper wisdom will guide our response to the assault on our inner abode. If the attack is a grossly physical one by a violent criminal, the body will have its own inbuilt resources of defence, but a greater wisdom will teach us when we may grapple with the assailant and when we should lie low. It need hardly be said that a calm acceptance of the criminal's fury is far wiser than any bodily response. But after he has wreaked his havoc, the concerted forces of the law will deal with the matter and in due course he will be apprehended, as much for his own good as for that of society. The victim is inevitably the loser no matter how prompt the arrest may have been, but if he is a person of awareness, he may learn much about himself and the priorities that had previously directed his life. If he can have seen and faced his own inadequacies and moved forth towards the light, his terrible encounter with naked violence will have borne a strangely productive fruit. Every experience has something to teach us about ourselves and the wider issues of life provided we have the patience and courtesy to listen rather than simply bemoan our lot and move on in bitter resentment. The same principle holds for the more common, less immediately dangerous attacks that are made on our personal integrity by jealous people. These would like nothing better than to undermine the happiness of those against whom they bear malice. In this respect, it is a sad fact of human nature that hatred of the oppressor often outdistances concern for the oppressed. The release of negative emotions, especially under the guise of morality or religion, is easy and of great immediate satisfaction.

The conservation and growth of positive attitudes, like concern, compassion and love, is a slow, bitterly humiliating process in which we seem to betray ourselves day by day. The further on we are in the quest for the precious pearl, the more insidious are the attacks of the evil one upon us. The road to heaven takes in large stretches of infernal landscape. If, however, the still point is attained and held during the heat of the day's encounters, the Holy Spirit can radiate from us, and produce a calming effect on the surrounding psychic atmosphere. A person who has this effect — one that comes from God and is emitted by the person, for it can never be produced by human will acting alone — is a true minister of healing. He is also a light on the path of the multitudes, who may begin to move away from the wide road that leads to destruction and edge towards the small gate that opens into the narrow road of eternal life.

Nothing persuades as forcibly as living example: Christ is shown in the lives of believers much more arrestingly than by their enthusiastic gestures and utterances. Indeed, the more vigorously we preach, especially when we denounce other people's beliefs, the more does our own naked insecurity reveal itself. When we work from the still point, we are in a wonderful way enabled to respect other points of view and assimilate from them what is helpful in our own journey. At the same time we can, by our very presence, show to others the inadequacies of those points of view. I am in this respect always in debt to St Augustine's statement:

> That which is called the Christian Religion existed among the Ancients, and never did not exist, from the beginning of the Human Race until Christ came in the flesh, at which time the true religion, which already existed, began to be called Christianity (*Librum de vera religione*, Chapter 10).

This true religion is often called the perennial philosophy or the ageless wisdom. It has in one way or another been taught by all the prophets and sages of mankind, whether eastern or western, but with Christ it took root in the world, which then entered upon its great course of resurrection, the end of which we still await with awe. It will coincide with Christ's coming again, this time in glory. Thus Augustine could in like fashion affirm that the Incarnation was the only Christian doctrine which he could not find in the Platonists.

To come back to a more mundane note, when we are assailed by the irritations and aggravations of the living world, our great test is not to return our own volley of abuse forthwith, but rather to return to the centre within the still point of a perilously gyrating universe, taking with us the clamour and confusion around us. This advice may seem strange; surely it would be better to rise above it all and let the stream of disorder rush on beneath our raised feet. But in real living we cannot exclude ourselves from the turmoil and unhappiness of others; indeed, any such movement of escape would soon be checked by even greater disorder impinging upon us from outside. Being so much parts of the one body of humanity, our psychic interrelatedness cannot but draw us back into the vortex of the storm until we have attained such mastery of our emotions that we can control our responses instead of having them overwhelmed by outside pressure. The test of the spiritual life is to know the presence of God at all times, especially when disorder strikes or, even more pertinently, when we are maliciously attacked, whether physically or, more commonly, verbally or psychically.

But what is the nature of the response from one who functions from the still point of the soul? There are two aspects of this response: an immediate calm acceptance without any trace of retributive violence, remembering the dictum, 'Vengeance is mine, says the Lord, I will repay' (Romans 12.19), and a more considered deliberation about the matter and the means to prevent, as far as possible, a recurrence of it. The latter is most important, for misdemeanours cannot be allowed to recur unchallenged, as much for the sake of the culprit as for ourselves and society at large. In other words, concern is far removed from sentimental compliance or a desire to cause as little disturbance as possible. This latter is an especially plausible way of evading personal responsibility, not only out of sheer indifference or laziness, but also from fear of being identified too closely with the retributive arm of the law. Since we are enjoined to forgive those who hurt us, not merely a few times, but indefinitely (Matthew 18.21-2), we may feel guilty at harbouring distrust against apparently penitent wrongdoers, especially if these happen to be in our own close circle. Forgiveness, however, does not mean turning a blind eye to bad behaviour, let alone criminal action. It does not annul the cause of justice, but softens its punishment according to the genuine repentance of the wrongdoer. Here there is a difference between the makeshift apology of the brazen offender, who is clearly trading on the finer feelings of his victim so as to escape the results of his evil actions, and the genuine penitence of the morally sensitive person, who has fallen, through his own weakness, into bad company and earnestly resolves a changed life in the future. The first must be handled with stern discipline, the second with protective firmness and loving concern so that his moral vulnerability may be strengthened against the temptations ahead of him in the battle of life. When one confronts the vast face of humanity, concentrated in one's own personality, one shudders at its weakness, and then is amazed at its potential nobility. Jesus' words from the cross, 'Father, forgive them; they do not know what they are doing' (Luke 23.34), ring out with timeless truth. Jesus' forgiveness is a blank cheque, but before we can take advantage of it we have to repent of the past and sincerely dedicate ourselves to a new life of service and decency. Only then do we know the power of that all-embracing forgiveness.

Thus from the point of stillness decisions can be made in quietness and strength. One of the inveterate problems that affects us all is the constant impingement of our emotions on our thought processes. Emotional thinking is often degrading to the subject and destructive to the object. To have our emotions under proper control so that they can fertilize our thoughts but not dominate them is an important part of spiritual growth. One way of approaching this task is to practise constant awareness and control of our own responses, saying and doing nothing without prior consideration. In this way we will not be subject to impulsive behaviour or intemperate language. The difficulty about this is that the spontaneity of natural existence is gradually sapped, while the ego consciousness assumes an increasingly dominant role. Everything that is said or done is purely for our own benefit — or what we confidently believe to be our benefit. The work of the Holy Spirit is diminished as he is increasingly cut out of our consciousness. To be sure, there are certain perilous situations in which a knife-sharp discretion is vital, and we dare not move beyond elementary safety, but it is a sad life where we cannot let go of our native reserve and allow the creative power of the Holy Spirit to guide us into a new and living way. Certainly there can be no growth into the knowledge of God without the infusion of his spirit into us, and this incurs a life of danger as well as safety. Each new confrontation with life provides an opportunity for growth.

In all four Gospels Christ tells us that we have to die to self in order to find the true being within us, the form of eternal life. A characteristic injunction is found in Mark 8.35-6;

> Whoever cares for his own safety is lost; but if a man will let himself be lost for my sake and for the gospel, that man is safe. What can a man gain by winning the whole world at the cost of his true self?

The point is made even more strongly in John 12.24-5;

> A grain of wheat remains a solitary grain unless it falls into the ground and dies; but if it dies it bears a rich harvest. The man who loves himself is lost, but he who hates himself in this world will be kept safe for eternal life.

Of course, Jesus speaks with the hyperbole of the impassioned spiritual teacher when he talks of self-hatred, and the grain of wheat falling into the ground dies only in its present form. Its life is continued in the shoot that emerges from it and eventually in the numerous seeds that will be shed from its flowering parts. The ego self is not in itself anything but good, since it is the vehicle of our individual expression in the noisy, brash world in which we are summoned to play our part. It is the servant of the personality, subject to change and ultimate death, similar to the body that contains it. The true self is situated in the spirit and the 'area' around it, the soul, which is the seat of moral discrimination and whose action is the will, free if unencumbered with emotional attachments that deflect it into unprofitable paths of action. The spiritual path is one of disengagement from the demands of the ego and a return to the soul where the still point is the place of reference, the precious pearl the destination, and the vision of God the constant, if unrecognized, companion. At this stage the ego is absorbed back into the soul, so that our individual expression is now a soul-inspired one and not the thrusting, assertive, egoistical outburst of the past.

This return to the centre of our being comes through the hard, pitiless testing of everyday living and the practice of prayer. The more consistently we can act from the still point within, the closer we are to the pearl and to the experience of eternity. This, rather than the practice of unceasing control of our responses, is the way in which we can be free from the bondage of our passions and the emotional outbursts that emanate from them. We cannot, if we are honest to our nature, simply rise above the aggravations of everyday life so that they cease to ensnare us. It is very fortunate for us that we cannot thus escape painful contact with the less agreeable facts of everyday existence. The contact may be aggravating, infuriating and deeply wounding, but when it has been surmounted in faith and courage, we will find that we have been loosed of some encumbrance of personality of which we had previously been unaware. Just as the sculptor fashions the image from the block of solid stone, so do the aggravations of relationships serve to excise ungainly excrescences of character and leave behind the well-proportioned form of a mature person. The process, needless to say, is a slow one, and the pain inflicted teaches us about the still point, where alone we can weather the storms with relative calm, until we learn by experience how to attain that blessed calm by an act of will. Here, in fact, we attain a knowledge of the confluence of divine grace and human free will. By grace we are led to the still point, by will we can repair there as occasion necessitates. Eventually, of course, we will find our constant abode there. If contemplation is one side of the coin of divine knowledge, active involvement in the world in deeper aware-ness of the present moment is the other. The more centred we are in our own identity, the more forcibly does our inner integrity assert itself as a quality in its own right, one not needing the assurance of recognition from others to affirm its own validity. Then indeed we can speak in truth, no longer being afraid either of the opinions of other people or of our own shadow side. In the still point shadow and direct consciousness come together as a whole unit. Nothing need therefore be hidden from view — ours as well as that of the world around us — any longer. I am reminded of a statement ascribed to a saint whose name escapes identity, 'I never knew peace until I had parted with my own reputation'. Whether these words are a true record or merely apocryphal, they speak volumes of truth about the human condition. The approval of other people is a dangerous idol if it deflects us from the course of action that we know is apposite. In fact, we attain far greater recognition by being true to our own particular insights than in attempting to smother them expeditiously in the cause of group solidarity. Our ultimate work is the repair of broken relationships, but this can be achieved only in an atmosphere of clear honesty. Incompatibilities of temperament, to say nothing of the demands for equity in a controversial situation cannot be bridged over by a simple formula of agreement. At the most such a formula may bring the parties together for a discussion, but until the requirements of justice have been met, there will remain a great gulf between them.

Does a spiritually enlightened person therefore cease to respond negatively to the irritations of those around him? He does indeed begin to attain this end, not so much by an act of deliberate will as by being increasingly filled with the Spirit of God whose nature is love. In this frame of mind we can indeed respond positively to the unequivocal injunctions against violence and resentment that resound from the Sermon on the Mount. This does not mean that we should bow our heads in servile submission to injustice, but that we should always be ready to communicate in warm faith with those who have hurt us, even if the intimacy of the conversation may not rise in strength above the level of heartfelt prayer for their repentance and healing. In such a manner the evil actions of unjust people wielding power can be parried with compassion, and our inevitable wounds may become a source of inner healing for ourselves as we, quite spontaneously, become representatives of the world's persecuted and oppressed. The way can at any time lead to death through the infuriated malice of our adversaries, but then at last death itself is seen in its broader context as a continuation of life on a more exalted level of experience.

Jean-Paul Sartre wrote that hell is other people; but hell is also complete isolation from human fellowship, an experience that hits us full in the face in our periods of loneliness. The situation reminds us of our relationship with the telephone: its frequent jarring calls can so disrupt our private life that we begin to resent its presence, but when it fails to register a dialling tone and cannot be used, we become anxious and dispirited until the fault is put right. Then we are truly thankful. Its unavailability cuts us off from the world, while its insistent presence cuts us off from our own inner composure where peaceful creativity finds its base. It is only when we are well centred in our own being that we can cope with the irritations of the outside world, neither shutting them out nor being overwhelmed by them. It is incidentally no bad thing to feel angry when our inner sanctuary is encroached upon by thoughtless people, who selfishly consume far too much of our precious time without even realizing how they are draining us. This anger is a mechanism of defence, and in due course it will serve to cut short depleting encroachments on our inner space, but when we are truly centred in the still point, the need for anger evaporates, as we find we can act with authority in any situation at any time. In a strange way, unprofitable interviews and telephone calls seem to find their own proper span of time and their moment of termination; we need neither reject the presence of other people nor depend upon it for our own security. When we are fixed in our own identity and centred in the still point we are both completely alone with God and in full communion with the whole world. In this situation our very life is a great intercession for the world and each individual living in it.

When I meditate on the life of Jesus, I see so much of his time spent with uncomprehending people — and his disciples seem to have been remarkably obtuse in understanding his message. Only after the pentecostal downflow of the Holy Spirit upon them, which ignited the Spirit within them, did they begin to grasp the universal significance of his incarnation. But Jesus surely also grew as a person in response to the aggravation he must so often have felt even at the intrusions of his own family during the course of his teaching ministry, so that at the end he could find peace between two criminals crucified on either side of him.

11 Powers and Principalities

St Paul, at the end of his letter to the Ephesians, reminds his readers that the fight is not against human foes, but against cosmic powers, against the superhuman forces of evil in the heavens. To an earth-attached liberal generation, these lurid terms of reference to cosmic evil do indeed seem far-fetched, but the very events of our own century cannot but bring us to a more cautious approach to reality. We do indeed live at a dangerous period in a very unstable society, in which anything might happen at any time. I often think of the concluding lines of W. E. Henley's poem, *Invictus*:

> It matters not how strait the gate,
> How charged with punishment the scroll,
> I am the master of my fate;
> I am the captain of my soul.

The poet was a vigorous atheist who lived at the end of the nineteenth century, when liberal ideals were coming to the fore in emancipated western society. Thus Alfred Tennyson could write of 'a land of settled government, a land of just and old renown, where freedom slowly broadens down from precedent to precedent'. The idea of a liberally orientated, evolving society, an evolution that was part of its very nature, similar to the Darwinian model of biological progress in which natural selection determined the onward flow of growth and differentiation of various species, seemed irresistible. The terrible events of our own century, in which two disastrous world wars were punctuated by the planned extermination of millions of humans, and the release of nuclear energy upon unsuspecting populations, have at least served to shatter these mechanistic, humanistic illusions, and as we approach the last decade of the twentieth century, we seem to be drawing breath just in time to avert a nuclear holocaust.

At the same time as these world events have shown us how little control we have over our lives and earthly destiny, the

103

work of Sigmund Freud and his numerous successors has revealed the fragmented consciousness by which we live day by day, even when there is peace and prosperity around us. Of course, the great Christian spiritual directors of the past knew about this — and we think again of Romans 7.14-25 where St Paul laments the tragic ambivalence of unredeemed human nature — but their voice has been largely drowned by the din of those who peddle earthly security, according to fashionable social and economic theories. The human is especially dangerous when he trusts in science to solve the enigma of life and believes that he can work out his own salvation by increasing his knowledge of the material universe and the process whereby it is maintained. We remember St Paul's famous words in 1 Corinthians 1.25, about divine folly being wiser than the wisdom of man and divine weakness stronger than man's strength. He is glorifying the amazing event of the resurrection that forms the high point of the doctrine of the cross, where failure on an earthly level is the precursor of a resurrection that involves not only Jesus but also all who follow in his way of life. I would hope nevertheless that Paul would not have purposely denigrated the achievements of scientific thought; he was speaking in terms of priority. Thus, when man can kneel in humility and thanksgiving before the Author of life, while affirming the enormous gains that scientific research has wrought, but remembering that none of this would have been possible but for the bounty of that Author, he sees himself in proper perspective as enlightened human agent working in devoted collaboration with the forces of goodness and love, the source of which is God himself.

While applauding all scientific endeavour that leads the mind to a greater grasp of truth, we begin to see that truth has no endpoint. The more we know, the greater our ignorance reveals itself. Thus we realize that no matter how expertly the scientist may unravel the basic processes involved in life and the very creative act itself, so that he may be able ultimately to define the elementary building block of the universe, he cannot explain how that basic particle (or whatever it may transpire to be) came into being. It is the spiritual alone that can create the physical, for the spiritual mode is eternal and of another realm of being as compared with the physical. This, by contrast, is finite, and subject to change, decay and destruction. But how can we know this spiritual realm, whose jewel is the precious pearl? It cannot be grasped with the reasoning mind because of its subtle nature. Instead it reveals itself to us when we are ready to receive it. The intimations that formed the beginning of this account are the way of revelation for the hardened materialist. To the less unobservant, more immediately aware, and those of humbler disposition, every moment of life reveals the spiritual foundation of existence: life itself is a miracle, something that induces wonder, as celebrated so gloriously by the writer of Psalm 139 who marvels at God's omnipresence, and the author of the Book of Job who celebrates the divine providence for all the creatures of the world in the great theophany that forms the zenith of the book.

But if a self-assured scientific humanism can lead us disastrously astray in the direction of hubris, a religious triumphalism can be equally detrimental in estranging us from the cool discriminating action of reason, so that we become captives to a man-made theory of God that can tolerate no dissention. It is no longer the desiccating intellect but the fervent emotions that take charge, leading not infrequently to a destructive fanaticism to which the many persecutions of minority, dissident groups in the world's chequered religious history bear a warning testimony. Indeed, the atheist has much truth on his side when he blames religion for most of the world's suffering. Unfortunately the events of our own century have shown that the good intentions of humanistic agencies are equally fatally flawed. All human schemes of social justice seem in the end to flounder as the individual takes advantage of a present opportunity for his own material benefit irrespective of the welfare of his fellows. This is a part of the original sin that we all inherit as the cross of human endeavour.

Humanistic endeavour without a spiritual base ends in truncating the human personality: intelligence and emotional drive are preserved, but there is no experience of a presence that leads us on from the restrictions of the world to the freedom of eternity. It was precisely for this experience of eternity that the human was created. He is to enjoy it and make it available for others; with it he emerges from his animal shell and advances triumphantly into the spiritual realm whose end is the vision of

God. Since, in the thought of St Augustine, God has made us for himself alone, and our souls are restless until they rest in him, there can be no ultimate fulfilment in a world of solid matter, until the soul soars heavenward in intimate communion with the divine. This is where the precious pearl is to be located, but as the pace of the journey quickens, so do dark shadows of menacing intensity cloud the way. These are no longer the little shadows that are part of the individual psyche, but a barely penetrable part of a dark, terrible conglomeration that works towards the annihilation of all that is good and pure. The still point of security is soon assailed by the demonic element in creation, and its simple repose rudely shattered. No one who moves heavenward can escape its impact, for it is the final barrier to be cleared before the pearl can be seen clearly. It seems that there is a force or power at the very root of the creative process that works towards its corruption and fall. Only the overthrow of all that is just, beautiful and conducive to the advancement of society in goodness and love will satisfy its Moloch-like greed. Like the Canaanite idol to whom children were sacrificed, it too thrives on all that is innocently good and pure, for lack of deeper knowledge. This is acquired only by experience, hence the necessity for a gradual approach to spiritual truth by the aspirant. The weak flesh that encompasses the willing spirit is only slowly strengthened until it can bear the assault of unmitigated evil and descend to the very depths of the infernal region. When we are most entrenched in our own security, the power of darkness is especially active. The terrible events of our own time bear dark testimony to a power of destructive malice that is cosmic in scope, yet capable of immense concentration in the individual psyche. It reaches its culmination in people who are naturally evil; they can be thought of as mediums of demonic activity. We have to face the unpalatable truth that there are evil geniuses in the world comparable in their destructive activities with the marvellous creativity inherent in scientific, artistic and spiritual geniuses. How they develop — indeed the reason for their very existence — is still a mystery, though genetic and environmental factors must surely play their part. I have, however, met a number of highly spiritually evolved people whose backgrounds have been so appalling that a criminal career would have appeared on the surface to have been inevitable. On the other hand, some frighteningly destructive people seem to have had all the social ingredients for a happy, constructive life. They are called psychopaths, but this categorization does nothing to explain their character. It is they who are especially powerful mediums of destructive cosmic forces, and their power is related to their intelligence and their ability to communicate on a psychic level with other people. The murderous type of dictator, so common in our century, typifies this trend to its most devastating extent.

The cosmic darkness is part of the intermediate psychic realm through which all communication between humans, as well as between them and God, takes place. It has been the fundamental error of the agnostic humanist of the past to ignore this dimension of reality, or else to believe fondly that its impact, if not its very source, could be neutralized and healed by liberal policies in education and economics. Ironically in fact, the destructive fury is animated primarily against all that is emancipated in thought and progressive in creativity and human relationships. Inasmuch as liberal attitudes refuse so often to confront the fact of naked evil or else to explain it away psychologically or sociologically, they are especially liable to provide a foothold for its actions until such time as they are protected by a powerful spiritual tradition that shows itself in prayer, worship and the life of charity. This is, in fact, the most cogent argument for religious education and ministry, remembering, as we have already observed, that religion can also go wrong and become the channel for demonic agencies. It must therefore be constantly monitored by tradition, reason, and above all the lives of its saints throughout the ages. These, to quote Hebrews 12.1, are the witnesses to faith around us like a cloud and with them we must throw off every encumbrance, every sin to which we cling, and run with resolution the race for which we are entered. The passage goes on to enjoin us to have our eyes fixed on Jesus, on whom faith depends from start to finish, who, for the sake of the joy that lay ahead of him, endured the cross, making light of its disgrace, and has now taken his seat at the right hand of the throne of God.

The evil that disfigures so much of our life on earth makes little outer impact on the man in the street. He is indeed shaken unobtrusively by its force, yet knows, like the crowd around Jesus on the cross, nothing of what he is doing or what is happening to him in the depths of his soul. The seeker of the pearl, however, as he approaches the end of his journey, is literally flattened by the onslaught of hatred and vile revulsion around him. It comes to him primarily as a psychic impact that aims at his total destruction. To this is added the secondary impact of human rejection and detestation. In the climactic events at Gethsemane and on the cross at Calvary the intensity of the onslaught was amplified. The evil is often channelled into the adversaries of the seeker, who by this time is no longer an anonymous private individual but a representative of the forces of light in a dark universe. He has emerged as a power with which to be reckoned, and the forces of controversy, jealousy and guilty fear tremble before him and then deliver the fateful blow. All this may sound forced and dramatic; in the instance of Jesus it delineates absolutely the genesis and development of the conflict between him and the powers of darkness in the world. These were concentrated in the political and religious leaders opposed to him, but it is important to understand that the drama was much more than merely a local conflict. It was a confrontation of cosmic extent. All humanity was involved in the crucifixion, so intimately are we all parts of the one body of creation. The collective sin of the world descended on those who condemned Jesus and called for his crucifixion. His Jewish brethren bear the stigma, but they were simply the local vehicle of the forces of destruction. They have become the scapegoats of a terrible miscarriage of justice, but like the tragic Judas Iscariot, they were also the hapless pawns of the powers of darkness that infest all rational creatures. Jesus' very perfection was the spark that ignited the conflagration of destructive hatred.

It follows that there are special agents of evil and also the general populace, who carry the torch from their leaders and set up an immense train of destruction. The evil impulse may well reside primarily among the fallen members of the angelic hierarchy. The legend of Lucifer challenging God and then excluding himself from the heavenly circle, so that his light, rendered false by his own wickedness, may now seduce all who are open to selfish impulses and malicious attitudes towards their fellows, seems to embody a truth, even if illustrated mythologically. The end of the powers of evil, wherever we may place their origin, is world domination. But behind this outer desire for conquest there is a hidden, deeper lust for total destruction. The evil impulse looks for the death of all life, the corruption of all beauty and the perversion of all truth and justice. Many types of violent agitators are similarly animated by their hatred of certain groups of humanity — if not all human beings — rather than their concern for the downtrodden and oppressed. The one who suffers the onslaught of evil may be tempted to hit back; resentment, hatred, and imprecations of vengeance all rear their heads in the Bible. Some of the psalms are full of cries for the destruction of the wicked, Psalm 109 being an especially notorious case in point. The apocalyptic books of both the Old and New Testaments likewise shower curses on the persecutors of the elect, and in some chapters of the Book of Revelation the hatred is of frightening intensity. The impulse to revenge is human enough, but the results of this type of writing have had lamentable repercussions in the form of persecutions centuries later. Only evil has triumphed.

On other occasions the train of evil is visited in a more personal way; the tribulations of Job are typical. Here a perfectly righteous man is suddenly deprived of wealth, family, health and, above all, the reputation that he so valued. In this story Satan is enabled to test Job to the utmost, provided that his life is spared. Though Job does not curse God, he does curse the day of his birth to his three friends who come to comfort him. To the burden of his sufferings he now has added the futile, pious platitudes of these three well-intentioned, but unimaginative visitors. They can be regarded as the prototypes of those who visit the sick and bring gloom and irritation with them, or those who telephone the convalescent patient to inquire about his health. Duty and curiosity rather than the intention of providing constructive assistance so often motivate their enquiries, which soon become an added burden that disrupts the patient's rest. All this the seeker of the precious pearl must learn to tolerate in addition to the pain of his humiliation and the suffering of his illness. In the drama of Jesus' crucifixion the only helpful spectators were the three women who stood patiently at the foot of the cross. They had no counsel to impart, only helpless love to give. Had Job's friends behaved likewise, they would have eased his burden instead of augmenting it. In other words, the hard impact of cosmic evil on the soul of the aspirant is aggravated by the emotional effusions of his fellows, ignorant rather than malicious. Only the one who has passed through the valley dark as death and has emerged into the light on the other side can be of help. The irony of the situation is the absence of such a helping hand in the travail of the seeker after truth. He, like Christ, has to proceed alone, deserted cruelly by his friends and apparently by God also. There is no outer prop any longer: faith itself is tested to its point of breaking, as all sources of hope recede into a background of dim memory and sad regret.

This does indeed seem to be the acid test of the probity of the seeker of the pearl: is he really prepared to sell everything he has in order to purchase it? Something more than money, time, inconvenience, reputation and personal relationships is demanded. It is his own self that he has to sacrifice, the self in fact that has to die before the true person can be revealed. The self that has sought the pearl is the ultimate price; not only are its outer comforts, those already mentioned, to be sacrificed, but also its intimate landmarks of identity. The most intimate landmark is one's own faith and the moral values on which it rests. All these are to be taken away — not because they are bad in themselves, which obviously is not true — so that the person may be shown completely naked before himself. He is, of course, always naked before God, as at the time of birth and death, as before the Fall and after it also, despite the contrivance of clothes to cover up Adam and Eve's private parts. But now nothing is left hidden between him and his fellows, him and God, and finally him and his own true being which is anchored in the soul. When he started out on the awesome journey to acquire the pearl he had no doubt that he would be ready to sacrifice all he possessed to attain his end. One sadly reflects on poor Peter confidently assuring his Lord, only shortly before the betrayal, that he at any rate would stand firmly beside him even if he had to die for him. Then only a little while later when Jesus was cruelly assailed by his enemies, Peter denied on three occasions ever having known the man. So in like manner the traveller to the kingdom of heaven has to be divested of everything that made him sure of himself, on which he fondly believed he could rely in complete trust. The reason for this radical disembarrassment of all outer attributes is that a cloud remains that blocks the way to the kingdom, that interposes itself defiantly between the seeker and the precious pearl, until the final act of renunciation.

St John of the Cross in *The Dark Night of the Soul* writes of 'dark contemplation', an enforced confrontation with the void that lies at the heart of all creation, a void so terrible in its absolute lack of limitation and termination that it seems to engulf and extinguish any hope for the future. It seems to annul any faith that there is anything at all for which hope could be a valid basis; yet the individual stands squarely in the void. It is in fact an authoritative confirmation of the immensity, the very totality, of the dark forces that have encompassed the creative process for at least as long as God's forward-looking creatures endowed with a reasoning mind have exercised their free but inexperienced, uninstructed wills. In our little world it is the human being that has been given dominion with immense power over his lesser brethren in the animal and vegetable worlds. Until they are schooled in awareness and grounded in charity, the human creatures are capable of fearsome cruelty applied with destructive energy to all this exists. And yet, strangely and confusingly, this capacity for destruction seems to be an integral part of the creative process. Without it, the creative impulse would lack an urgent stimulus for advance, and the growth of the individual would be stultified, eventually grinding to a final halt. It seems that somehow a balance has to be struck between the forces of creative evolution and those of destruction until a new creature of promise is conceived from their tempestuous union. It is precisely this new birth into reality that the seeker of the pearl of great price has dedicated himself to attain, though he would never have conceived what it entailed, indeed its very nature, at the outset of his apparently praiseworthy but innocuous journey. He is now poised at the very centre of the vortex of creation, and has offered himself as a lamb of sacrifice for the great work of human evolution. He has expanded from a minute particular to embrace the world, but it is a world, as St Paul puts it so unforgettably in Romans 8.21-2, groaning in all its parts as if in the pangs of childbirth. And so he too suffers the terrible pain of creation breaking free of the destructive power that checks it, to enter into that freedom from the shackles of mortality and enter upon the liberty and splendour of the children of God. And the seeker has now graduated to the position of a truly awakened child of God who can help his Father in the ceaseless process of creation.

The seeker has offered himself indeed as the sacrificial lamb in unwitting imitation of the Lamb of God who was sacrificed from the creation of the world. Christ sacrifices himself perpetually on the altar of human cruelty, so that in the end his way may form a bridge between the human and the divine, bridging even the gulf between the sacred and the profane, the saint and the sinner. The seeker may have previously read all this in texts from Scripture and the great spiritual writers of mankind, and even been strangely inspired by their power, but now he finds himself in the crucible of purification where text assumes the reality of existence. He is now being finely purged of all personal attachments, all illusions that stand in the way of the vision of God. To these are added the collective idolatries of the society from which he has sprung.

At last he is truly nothing, the grain of wheat that is in process of dying, the sacrificial lamb slain to save his fellow creatures from death, not by propitiating God's anger but by giving of himself, now sanctified, for their enlightenment. For a moment he can see the precious pearl quite clearly though apparently a long way off; then all is occluded from his vision.

12 Behold the Man

The final act of the drama of life is played out. All that has
preceded it seems in retrospect to have been a preparation for
the last test. The dim intimation of time beyond recall, followed
by the direct act of will to choose the way to the pearl which had
the secret of life engrained in it, was in turn succeeded by a
deeper knowledge of the darkness within the personality.
When the confrontation of the shadow existence was well nigh
intolerable, the mysterious God showed himself in the cloud as
well as the light. Acceptance of the darkness within revealed
how hollow one's intentions were, and how crudely self-
centred one was, even in the pursuance of holy objectives. This
in turn brought with it the inner injunction to give oneself
entirely to the present moment, since in that moment the vision
of the pearl was most clearly revealed, and that healing of the
inner baseness could take place only by divine grace assisted by
an aware, chastened will. The temptations of esoteric exploration were confronted, tasted and by-passed inasmuch as they
led up a blind alley; the scepticism of contemporary thought
was bowed to but surmounted by a faith more dark than
enlightened. This, in turn, led to the still point of the soul from
whose vantage one could see the limitation of the unenlight-
ened reason, and find strength in the peace of God. But this rest
was not granted one for too long, lest a dreamy complacency
diverted one from the greater quest. Thus the aggravations of
the daily scene, the common round, assailed one, reminding
one of one's involvement with the whole of human society no
matter how far one's personal vision had seen beyond its
corporate desires and objectives.

Then, just as a fresh relationship with the encompassing
world had been attained, one was abruptly jolted out of a new
complacency by the assault of the forces of cosmic darkness.
The battle was almost lost in its vicious intensity, but then in the
total darkness the pearl was seen with a radiance hitherto
unknown. The journey is indeed drawing to its end, but now

comes the final test.

It comes to all of us who have offered ourselves to the good life — not so much one of piety as of positive relationships with our fellows coruscating in the jet of love, at first to single individuals but progressively to all humanity. God asks us whether we are prepared to give up everything for his sake, and our response reveals our integrity of will and intensity of purpose. When the ultimate demand is made, it is important that we should flinch from it in horror. If it were to be obeyed with too great an alacrity, it would show a shallowness of emotional response rather than a trembling obedience, heavy with foreboding and dark in mental anguish as the way unfolded. We consider Jesus' dictum, reiterated in one way or another by the collective witness of the world's saints, that whoever cares for his own life is lost, but that if he will let himself be lost for the highest good, he will attain a safety that can never be impugned. It is the ego self that has to be surrendered before the true identity of the soul with its spiritual centre can be revealed; the soul's integrity is assured because of that spiritual centre, where God is known. God leads the soul to new heights of endeavour until all its labours are lifted up to the divine essence. Nevertheless, it is very hard to yield the ego identity with the physical body that serves it. This is not so much due to human ignorance as to the working of the divine will. The ego and the physical body are essential components of the personality while we do our work on earth during the brief space of time given us, for even a hundred years of life are as nothing in the eternity of God. This is not to be transcribed even in terms of the unfathomable millions of light-years reckoned by the astronomer. Eternity, on the contrary, lies outside the time scale. It is a completely different experience of reality, but, once glimpsed, throws a radically new light on the creative process and human destiny.

While, however, we are constrained by the experience of time and space, our identity is limited by these parameters. This is no loss, for we are here to learn humility and practicality by the very restrictions they impose upon us. We have to learn to love the world and, even more cogently, to love ourselves with all our human deficiencies. Only that which is loved can provide a proper sacrifice for God. Only the loved thing can be of transforming service to his creation. It, no matter how trivial its value and unpretentious its form in the world's eyes, is made sacred by love. It then becomes a fit offering of our very lives to that which so dwarfs us in its magnitude that we could scarcely envisage ourselves as being registered by it in its magnificence. Love elevates all objects to the divine form; it consecrates them to God's service, thereby making them holy; thus they are sanctified. In the account, in Mark 12.41-4, of the widow's mite, the meaning of sacrifice is perfectly expounded in respect of a trifling sum of money: the widow's minuscule gift comes from her heart and has seriously impoverished her, whereas the substantial contributions of the wealthy have a distant, perfunctory air about them. While in no way to be dismissed, since they have obvious material value, they are not radiated by a love that alone can redeem riches from their seditious role in preventing spiritual growth: the security they promise can so easily dampen the impulse to helping forward the kingdom of God. Indeed, the essential purpose of our life on earth is to love the world, its manifold creatures, and ultimately, and most exacting in intensity, to love ourselves in our entirety. Only then can we give of ourselves in unstinted service as we lose ourselves in love and know a death of the acquisitive part of our personality that unfolds into the resurrection of the true personality, at once of childlike innocence and wise experience. We are to return to the image of God implanted in the soul, but now strengthened and affirmed by the experience of temptation, fall, despair and renewed hope in the face of apparently insurmountable difficulties.

The supreme sacrifice to God is ourself, and it is given freely not to God's need but to the service of our fellow creatures. The sacrificial ritual of the Mosaic covenant, which was continued in the temple up to the time of Christ and its final destruction some seventy years after his birth, fills us today with revulsion, and justly so. But the people were being taught in the early days of their spiritual apprenticeship that all things belong to God and that man is a mere steward during his time on earth. If an animal was sacrificed in love and gratitude, it brought the human closer to the divine presence. But the real sacrifice is a broken spirit and a wounded heart, as the greatest of the Penitential Psalms teaches (51.17). As Amos fulminated against impeccable ritual animal sacrifice in the face of social injustice, so Hosea taught that God required loyalty and a true knowledge of himself, not killed animals (Hosea 6.6). Nevertheless, inner attitudes can remain blissfully oblivious of outer demands until they are incarnated in acts of charity and service. As animal sacrifice recedes into the mist of history, so does personal sacrifice assume an ever more central position. Then do we reveal our true nature; then does the pearl come into unobstructed view.

The final test in the eventful life of that scriptural representative of faith, Abraham, is the divine command to sacrifice his son Isaac, who not only is a greatly beloved child, but is also chosen to carry forward the creative work of the children of God. The story is conspicuous for its starkness of detail and absence of any recorded emotional response on the part of the patriarch (Genesis 22.1-14) to the terrible commission, but the mention of the love he has for his son speaks more eloquently of his inner desolation than any more detailed description. It is interesting that as the book of Genesis proceeds, so do the emotional responses of the participants become more prominent. We think of the terror of Jacob as he, after many years absence, has to confront his wronged brother Esau once more; he is a wanderer, while Esau is now a powerful chieftain, who could destroy him and his retinue with a stroke of the hand. Jacob has to face the full impact of his past life alone, after sending all his dependants across the ford of Jabbok. Wrestling with the accusing angel of God, who is remarkably ambivalent in moral character, so that he resembles the accuser Satan of the Job story quite as much as an obedient servant of God (such as Abraham had met on several occasions during his earthly life), he has to face himself in the glass of God. Compared with this confrontation, the meeting with Esau pales into insignificance. Nevertheless, Jacob passes the test without flinching or cringing behind a servile piety that seeks to deflect the attack. He has, after all, outgrown the deceitfulness of his youth and revealed the strength of a mature man. He prevails and obtains a blessing so that his name — and therefore his nature — registers a change of stature. He is one who has contended with God, which is the probable meaning of Israel. Now he has attained the spiritual authority of a patriarch, but his hip is permanently out of joint. It is his wound, comparable in its own context to the stigmata of the risen Christ revealed to Thomas, to assure him of the Lord's authenticity. Resurrection can only succeed crucifixion, just as mastery comes at the end of a long period of trial. This is indeed the test of a spiritual master; by comparison, esoteric knowledge is superficial and largely irrelevant. He has at last grasped the pearl, knowing that it is real and not simply a spiritual illusion, a will-o'-the-wisp that fades out of sight as it is directly approached.

In the story that concludes the book of Genesis, that of Joseph and his brethren, the emotional aspect is very prominent. Indeed, without this response such towering spiritual themes as obedience, sacrifice and forgiveness would lack authenticity. The human agent would then be reduced to the status of a puppet. There has to be a struggle between the claims of the ego that seeks immediate justice and compensation, and the soul that, being directed by the Spirit of God, lives increasingly in an atmosphere of love. Furthermore, both attitudes have to be acknowledged; the ego cannot be summarily dismissed nor its demands contemptuously swept aside as a juvenile regression, unworthy of the mature personality. But as the spiritual path is trod, so the ego is gradually trained to set its sights beyond immediate, unabashed gratification to a deference for natural justice. This is an important step on the path of its transmutation, but not the end of the journey. The final movement leaves behind all demands for personal satisfaction. Its end is an open, unconditional acceptance of life in a spirit of forgiveness and deep compassion for all that lives. The journey is, in fact, one that leads to the precincts of the precious pearl. It is long-extended and not to be rushed or expedited by any procedure that obscures basic moral issues. In other words, truth is not sacrificed in the interests of love. It is, however, extended in range when it is informed by love. In such a climate of enlightened love and impassioned honesty Jesus' injunctions against judging and condemning other people become intelligible to the point of lucidity.

In this way the saint, who is potentially each of us when we attain full awareness of each moment in time in prayer to God and service to our fellows, is able increasingly to accommodate within himself the sins of those around him. He can, with the patient love of a true parent, accept the shortcomings of his friends, even assimilating them into his own psyche by an act of spiritual substitution: he takes up the other person's darkness which he then places on the altar of his heart (or the altar of a church) as his sacrifice to God, who not only accepts it, but also transfigures it into something of the glorified wounds of Christ. This is a very different way of dealing with the sinner than the customary practice of endeavouring to put right what is wrong, according to our own judgement. While such an approach may be imperative in the short term, its effects are liable to be of limited duration until a radical change in heart has been brought about. This can be effected by God alone; he works through the love of those who serve him in constant devotion and care for their fellow creatures. The sacred child is not at home in the edifice of pure reason that finds its point of reference in a court of law or a university lecture theatre. As T. S. Eliot writes in *East Coker*:

> To arrive where you are, to get from where you are not,
> You must go by a way wherein there is no ecstasy.
> In order to arrive at what you do not know
> You must go by a way which is the way of ignorance.
> In order to possess what you do not possess
> You must go by the way of dispossession.
> In order to arrive at what you are not
> You must go through the way in which you are not.
> And what you do not know is the only thing you know
> And what you own is what you do not own
> And where you are is where you are not.

This way of negative unfolding, classically expounded by St John of the Cross, is the final demand made on us as we prepare to claim the precious pearl. It then suddenly eludes our grasp though within bare contact of our hands. The darkness that had previously lifted from our gaze suddenly descends on us with the impenetrability of a dense fog. All visible and tangible landmarks are submerged in the gloom as we call out in vain for someone to rescue us. When Abraham prepared to sacrifice Isaac he was stopped just before the fateful act by God, and a ram caught by its horns in the thicket proved an acceptable substitute, but in the great test, there is no such substitute as we enter the final stretch. We, like Jesus, are the sacrifice, and unless, like him, we are prepared to play the man, all our endeavours will have been in vain. Even he could have failed: if not, his humanity would not have been similar to ours. But, he stayed the course to the end, an end shrouded in lamentable tragedy and failure to those who watched the unfolding of the crucifixion drama from the safety of the ground of the cosmic theatre. We all in every age are these spectators until we hear and obey his eternal call, 'Follow me'.

Our own century, hemmed in by tyrannies which would have seemed inconceivable to our recent forebears, who looked with great confidence for the unfolding evolution of human society to increasingly liberal thought and enlightened social concern, has yielded its quota of martyrs for the cause of righteousness. The basis of martyrdom, as the Greek origin of the word indicates, is a bearing witness to the truth, at least as one personally sees it, even to the sacrifice of one's own life. Most martyrdom has an unashamedly partisan flavour about it, as when a 'freedom fighter' goes to his death in the furtherance of his ideals; there is little love for his adversaries in his action, which in fact is very strongly coloured by anger and hatred. The martyrdoms described in the Second Book of Maccabees, notably 6.18-31, 7.1-42 and 14.37-46, are classics of this type. Without, however, this intensity of commitment, the Jewish religion would have been completely crushed by the hellenizing policy of Antiochus Epiphanes. The same is surely true of much early Christian martyrdom in the time of the Roman persecutions: the flame was kept alive, but there was no concession made to the souls of the heathen. This lack of charity has its backlash in the course of history: battles may be won on the worldly level, but ideologies, after lurking unobtrusively in the background during the period of persecution, tend to reassert themselves, perhaps centuries later, when the climate of opinion is more favourable for their propagation. Thus paganism is once again rife in western society.

A truly spiritual martyrdom, paradoxically it would seem, does not work towards the end of supreme sacrifice. This is the greatest love that is prepared to give up its life for its friend, who ceases to be merely an isolated person but instead embraces the whole body of mankind, though in practice an individual may stand as a representative of the whole human situation. On the contrary, self-sacrifice is thrust upon the aspirant as a by-product of his increasing awareness and spiritual proficiency. This is seen in a deeper, more intense prayer life and an ever more rounded, equable disposition in the face of the surrounding social chaos. Such a person is not a fanatic like the all-too-familiar freedom-fighting terrorist who, as we have already noted, is inflamed with hatred, no matter how justified this may appear to the impartial observer, against his antagonist. To be sure, the aspirant may have started his spiritual search on such a zealous note, but, as he progressed in spiritual discipline he would have discovered that he contained within himself all the unacceptable qualities he so eagerly tended to project on to his enemies. But for God's grace he too might have followed their example. Thus the blinding self-righteousness of the fanatic, the terrorist and the religious bigot is gradually lightened by compassion born of understanding and suffering. His exemplar is Jesus himself, whether or not he knows the name or claims the association. This final act crowns a lifetime's spiritual discipline, without which he would not have had the capacity to do the work in the spirit of love and forgiveness.

But as the journey to the pearl reaches its objective, the person is stripped bare: his final payment is himself, and now he stands revealed to the world. His antecedents, his very origin, may be shrouded in mystery, but at last he has attained the glow of world recognition and is a flame of the light that illuminates the world, the light of Christ himself. After Pilate had cross-questioned Jesus, found him essentially guiltless of the charges laid against him, but was about to hand him over to the religious authorities to wreak their own vengeance upon him, he first had him flogged, crowned with thorns and robed in a purple cloak. After Jesus had been humiliated by the attending soldiers, Pilate again presented him to the people, affirming once more his conviction of his innocence. He said, 'Behold the man', as he gave him over to be crucified (John 19.1-5). Each of us has to face this terrible exposure, some in a dramatic situation encompassing earthly life, but all eventually at the moment of death. On the negative side we remember Peter's thrice-repeated denial of his master. We recall David's seduction of Bathsheba and the subsequent murder of her husband Uriah the Hittite which were brought into critical focus by the prophet Nathan, who roundly denounces his shameless lust and cruelty. We shudder at Ahab's cold-blooded destruction of Naboth in order to seize his vineyard, only to be met by Elijah, who pronounces a terrible fate on his posterity. Each is shown himself in the mirror of truth, and the reflection is repulsive to behold.

We hope that the reflection of ourselves that we are in process of fashioning will be less forbidding in our latter days. It may even reveal something of the beauty of a saint, if we have followed the path to the pearl in honest endeavour and humble service, but we cannot know until the final show. What have we to offer at the bar of judgement? What have we made of the life given us by God, so that when we return home at the end of the day, he may say to us, 'Well done, my good and trusty servant! You have proved yourself trustworthy in a small way; I will now put you in charge of something big. Come and share your master's delight' (Matthew 25.21)? Let us contemplate the supreme acts of self-sacrifice of some of our chequered century's spiritual giants. There was, for instance, Mother Maria Skobtsova, an emigrée Russian-Orthodox nun who lived in France after the communist take-over. She spent her time caring for the inmates of prisons and mental hospitals, living in great poverty, sharing all the privations of the downtrodden and outcasts and confirming their own precious identity in her witness. But her shining hour followed the German occupation, when she dedicated herself to helping the Jews. In due course she was arrested by the Nazis, and sent to a concentration camp where she died a martyr's death in the gas chambers in April 1945: she changed places with a young Jewish mother.

Another heroic exchange in a concentration camp is exemplified in the death of Maximilian Kolbe, a Polish Catholic priest, now canonized by his Church. In the case of Dietrich Bonhoeffer, who belonged to the Protestant wing of the German Church, we have a man who rebelled increasingly against the Nazi ethos to the point of taking part in a plot against the lives of the political leaders of that evil regime. This he did in order to curtail the suffering that the war which they engineered had brought upon the nation no less than its numerous victims and adversaries. The propriety of using assassination as a means of ridding the world of depraved people is always open to question, and in fact the plot was uncovered. All its participants were mercilessly killed, so that a martyr's death saw the fruition of Bonhoeffer's work of reconciliation. I do not believe that he detested the Nazi leaders personally but rather was revolted at the extent of the evil they perpetrated. However, in our imperfect world we cannot forgo the use of force to deal with criminals, whether domestic, national or international.

On other occasions the supreme sacrifice has been less dramatic but equally impressive as a witness to the truth. We think, for instance, of the German Jewess Edith Stein who became a Carmelite nun, Sister Teresa Benedicta of the Cross. Transferred to a Dutch convent early in the Nazi regime, she became a victim of Hitlerite persecution following the German occupation in Holland. When the local Catholic clergy protested against the persecution of the Jews — Holland has always had a splendid reputation for kindness to its Jewish community — Sister Teresa Benedicta was summarily transported to the gas chambers of Auschwitz concentration camp, where her equanimity was an inspiration to many of her fellow victims. Unlike the previous saints that we have mentioned, she did not deliberately give up her life for anyone; rather, her martyrdom was a witness to the fundamental decency of human nature in the face of its dark, bestial propensities. Another German Jew, Leo Baeck, showed another facet of martyrdom. He was a rabbi of the Liberal Jewish Synagogue. Imprisoned in a foul concentration camp, he brought strength and purpose to his fellow victims by initiating a study of the Greek influence on Judaism. Even at the worst times he showed no resentment, and when he was amazingly liberated at the end of the war, he refused to visit vengeance on his squalid gaolers. A few years later, shortly before his death, he visited Germany in a spirit of loving reconciliation. How easy it would have been for him to have shown contempt for his erstwhile persecutors! In a way, this type of witness shows quite as much love as that of the person who sacrifices his life for someone else. Death is kinder than the harrowing torture of the human frame in the prison camps of our 'advanced' twentieth century. The forgiveness re-echoes the words of Christ on the cross of human cruelty.

The witness need not necessarily be to an outer atrocity; the terror may lie within. A notable Hindu saint of our century, Sri

Ramana Maharshi, continued his great work of prayer, healing
and teaching as his mortal body was slowly destroyed by
cancer. His radiance flowed out to all living forms, and his
influence on the spiritual life of many people has been unequal-
led in its purity and love. As I have already said, we each have to
prepare an account of our lives at some fateful juncture. The
great ones have moved beyond self-concern to a free self-giving
to the world. The one who claims the pearl of great price,
paradoxically, is no longer there to receive it in outward form.
He has, in naked purity, merged with it as its radiance enfolds
him.

13   The Assumption of the Pearl

As the aspirant makes his final show in the theatre which is our world, standing naked for all to behold his powerlessness in the face of ignominy and despair, so he becomes aware of a body of ghostly spectators approaching him from the mists of eternity. They do not, in fact, so much move towards him as stand in firm array to watch over him. Their support is one of witness. They in their time also faced the evil powers of the world and stood steadfast, grounded in their faith as they witnessed to the reality of spiritual values: they served in love despite the blind incomprehension of all those who lived alongside them. Their victory is the form of support that they bring to their hard-pressed brother, but now it is no longer a tale but a living presence.

As the scene widens, so the encompassing forces of darkness fade into the distance, as they are gradually supplanted by people beyond measure, the whole body of mankind, and eventually the entire created universe, who watch with bated breath as the postulant surmounts the final barrier to take his place among the body of the immortals. These are the crown of the Communion of Saints, of whom even we little ones on this side of death are members, albeit mere fledglings as compared with the great saints, who have illuminated the annals of human history with a radiance of a different order from temporal power or imperial splendour. They are all of the race of martyrs, even if some were spared the terrible death of torture at the hands of an encompassing evil power that is the classical end of martyrdom. All bore witness to the noble face of God in mankind in their victory over the limitations of the mortal body and the corruption of the social institution in which they found themselves. Their witness inspired the human race and played its part in the civilization of the world.

St Irenaeus said that the glory of God is a man fully alive. The paradigm of this fully alive person is the saint; in Christian thought Jesus is the supreme witness. The affirmation that our

124

developed western world needs so desperately is that the human is a spiritual being; in the eastern world this is accepted as a matter of fact, but the squalid poverty of the masses belies this comfortable assumption. The martyrs have all in their own witness given proof of human spirituality, as they moved onwards to claim the prize at the end of the day: the pearl of great price for the sake of which they had not spared themselves or withheld their very lives.

The victorious ones pass without form from the life of the world to the void of eternity. This is the great cloud of unknowing which supported the Israelites day by day in the wilderness, and into which the spiritual body of Jesus advanced and was taken up as he left the limited atmosphere of our world at the time of his ascension to the centre of the divine power. 'A grain of wheat remains a solitary grain unless it falls into the ground and dies; but if it dies, it bears a rich harvest.' We have considered these words before; now at last their impetus attains its full impact. The witnesses to the truth have disappeared from view in their mortal form, only to reappear enshrined in the light of eternity. Theirs is a radiance that can never be extinguished because at the centre of their being there lies the pearl. From it the Light of the World shows himself. The saint now has the pearl enshrined within himself, and he has been transfigured: all that was mortal and perishable is now taken up in the eternal radiance of the pearl. Each of God's creatures has the potentiality of becoming a pearl in its own right; it is the privilege of the rational agent, in our world the human being, to work towards the transformation of the whole of creation so that it may actualize its fullness, even to becoming a pearl in the glory of God. Thus all is taken up into the precious gift of God, so as to become a fulfilment of that very gift. 'Then the Lord shall become king over all the earth; on that day the Lord shall be one Lord and his name the one name' (Zechariah 14.9).

When the saint attains his apotheosis, when the pearl illuminates him to a transparency that reveals God, the law of love attains its fulfilment. Then at last it becomes impossible to set oneself against the person who does one harm; it becomes a matter of course to turn the other cheek to the assailant, to give freely when called on to do so, and to accept without demur the demands of the stronger party. But now all resistance is gone, all sense of grievance annulled, as one flows out quite spontaneously in love to one's enemy and prays for one's persecutor. When one is the pearl, one has a single burning desire: to bring the pearl to others also: 'You are light for all the world . . . And you, like the lamp, must shed light among your fellows, so that when they see the good you do, they may give praise to your Father in heaven' (Matthew 5.14-16). What would have been impossible to the unaware person, and painfully jarring to the one on the path, now becomes an inevitable attitude in a new way of living. The saints in this world and the next work with constant devotion towards the transformation of society and the enlightenment of its individual members.

We find that the pearl resides in the spirit of the soul, in the depth of the personality of each one of us. When it is claimed, it shines radiantly within us, and from us to the world. It is seen by those around us in our daily work, but sheds a universal light during our times of prayer. And eventually prayer should never leave us, attaining constancy and ardour even during the most exacting work in the world.